STORYTELL
A practical guide

Lance Pierson

Scripture Union

Scripture Union, 207–209 Queensway, Bletchley, MK2 2EB, England.

© Lance Pierson 1997
First published 1997

ISBN 1 85999 094 0

Unless otherwise attributed, scripture quotations are from The Youth Bible, New Century Version, copyright © 1991 by Word Publishing, Dallas, Texas 75039. Used by permission.

British Library Cataloguing-in-Publication Data
A catalogue record for this book is available from the British Library.

Cover design by Rafale Design.
Cover illustration by Michelle Poultney.
Printed and bound in Great Britain by Cox & Wyman Ltd, Reading.

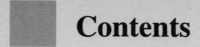# Contents

The story behind
Storytelling

Scripture Union asked me if I thought there was a need for a book on storytelling.

I thought of the stories that have been part of my life. Perhaps my all-time favourite is Dodie Smith's *The One Hundred and One Dalmatians*. My mother read it to me in hospital after I'd had my appendix out when I was ten. This was the original story before Walt Disney got hold of it. I laughed so much I was in stitches. Or rather, out of them! They had to redo the dressing on my scar.

I thought of our group at church for 7–11 year-olds. When they get restive, one of the leaders tells them the day's Bible story. You can see them go quiet with fascination. It almost never fails.

I thought of the college lecturer who told me about the latest discovery made by post-modernist communicators. 'It's no good trying to persuade people with reasoned arguments and lectures today,' he said. 'The way to get through to them is with stories.' And I thought, 'Surely the wisdom of the ages (not to mention Jesus, the master storyteller) knew this already!'

So I said to Scripture Union, 'Yes, we could do with a book on storytelling. Definitely' – which was rash of me. They asked me to write it, and I said OK – which was even more rash of me.

I thought again of all the stories that have been part of my life. Of all my attempts to teach the Bible and preach the good news with stories. And of everything that's happened to me when I've tried. And got stuck. How to sort it all out? How to make sense of it? And how to help you, the reader, make sense of it?

Someone said to me, 'Why not just tell your own storytelling story – how you started, what you learnt, why you still do it?'

So this is how it has turned out. The stories I quote are not great examples of the art. They are just stories which have meant a lot and had a big impact on me.

Each chapter marks a stage in my own journey as a storyteller – childhood and what I discovered about telling stories to children, the teenage years and what I learnt when trying to tell stories as a Scripture Union schools worker, experiments in teaching the faith to adults through stories as a lay preacher, and so on.

Life goes through these different stages and chapters, but you don't start each chapter with a blank sheet of paper. You carry over all the lessons you learnt in the earlier stages. So most of the tips in chapter one for telling stories to children still apply, with slight adaptation, when we tell stories to teenagers and adults. But I have not wasted space by repeating them in chapters two and three. I assume you have already mastered them – or are still working on them! Chapters two and three introduce new material to build on what you have discovered already.

In the same way, when chapter two explores parables, this is not because I think they are *only* relevant to teenagers. The ideas there work equally well, with suitable adaptation, for adults. It's just that I learnt most about parables when I was working with teenagers. This was the new ingredient I added to what I'd already learnt about storytelling.

I hope you can find your way round this book. And, more important, I hope it will help you tell more and better stories. If so, please join me in thanking those people who helped behind the scenes. Their comments have given vital twists to the book's own story. So roll the credits, please, for:

- Anna de Lange, Veronica Heley, Brenda Rogerson, Steve Stickley, Jeremy Thomson and Christine Wright.

- The Fellowship of Christian Writers Non-fiction Postal Workshop: Hazel Bradshaw, Anne Chandler, Kathleen Fry and Philippa Marshall.

- Chris and Marjorie Idle, and the Fellowship of Christian Writers Inner London Area Group.

- Alison Barr, Josephine Campbell and Tricia Williams, those most patient, encouraging and creative editors at Scripture Union.

Lance Pierson

1 Stories for children

What was your favourite Bible story as a child?

Mine was Jesus' parable of the lost sheep. Not that I knew it was a 'parable', nor that Jesus had told it. I only knew it as it appeared in *Blandford's Very First Bible Stories*. I asked my mother to read it to me again and again. Try to think back to when you were four or five...[1]

> Once there was a little black lamb who lived with his mother in a field...
>
> Sometimes the little black lamb got tired of the field. Then he would climb the wall which went round the field, where some of the stones had fallen, and look into the next one.
>
> The little black lamb thought the next field looked much nicer than his field. The buttercups looked bigger, and the grass looked very thick and green.
>
> 'Baa-baa! Don't ever go into that field,' his mummy would say, 'or you might get lost'...
>
> But one day, when he went to look over the wall, he saw it was easy to climb over into the next field, so he put one little hoof on the wall, then the other, and gave a little hop and jumped right down into the field.
>
> Just for a moment he felt frightened and he stood quite still to see if his mummy had noticed and was calling him.
>
> But she wasn't. She was with all the other sheep, all talking about their lambs with their heads close together; and she never even noticed that he had gone...
>
> And so he went on and on, farther and farther away from home...

At last, he began to get tired, and he thought he would go home ... but he could not remember the way. The ground grew rough and stony as he scrambled up and down, and the brambles caught in his black wool. At last he fell and cut his leg...

Away back in the field, the shepherd was looking around him and counting all the sheep and the lambs before bed-time.

'Where's my little black lamb?' he asked. 'I can't see him anywhere.'

'Baa-baa! We don't know,' the little black lamb's mummy said. 'I think he must have run away'...

'I'll go and look for him,' said the shepherd. 'I love your little black lamb too. Stay there, all of you, till I come back.'

So he left them and started out, carrying a lamp in his hand, and went looking and looking everywhere for the little black lamb. At last he heard a little voice crying, 'Meh-meh!'

'I'm sorry I ran away,' said the little black lamb. And he really was sorry.

'You won't ever do it again, will you?' said the shepherd, as he tied his handkerchief round the little lamb's leg.

'No,' the little lamb promised. 'No, I never will again.'

Then the shepherd picked up the little lamb in his arms, and the lamb thought he had the kindest, most loving face he had ever seen. Who do you think the shepherd was? Why, Jesus, of course!

The story is of its age. Politically incorrect now to make the lost sheep a naughty black runaway. Educationally dubious to make Jesus a character in an animal story. Morally unsound to make a 'child' promise never to do wrong again.

But none of that worried me. I simply gained an overpowering sense that Jesus loved me; that he went on loving me even when I was bad; that he wanted me to be good; that he would look after me; that he could give me a happy ending.

All this came straight from the story. But there was something else as well. This 'something' was mysterious and I couldn't fully grasp it. Somehow a third person came into the room alongside my mum and me as I snuggled up to her. Jesus was there too. And, although I didn't know how, I felt I could love him and trust him for myself. This is the powerful effect Bible stories can have.

All stories have an irresistible power. They trigger our creative imagination to enter the world of the story and become part of it. We see, feel and become part of the action. We stand beside the characters we like, willing them to come out on top; we recoil from the people we dislike, longing for them to meet their doom. And in the process we build our view of life. Sometimes the story confirms us in the attitudes we already hold; but sometimes it challenges us and opens us up to new possibilities.

Christian stories – and, supremely, Bible stories – do all this and more. They show us God's way of looking at the world. They help us feel how he feels when people are kind or cruel, brave or brash, happy or hopeless. And because God is present and active in his world, they help us find him there.

This is what we can expect to happen for children as we open Bible stories up to them.

The parable went underground in my subconscious. Over twenty years later, when I began to give all-age talks, I found myself attracted to Jesus' sayings about sheep and shepherds: 'I am the good shepherd' and 'I am sending you out like sheep among wolves' (John 10:11,14; Matt 10:16). I didn't consciously remember the little black lamb story, but I invented a 'Christian' lamb called Montmorency who featured in several stories.

In fact, now I come to think about it, Jesus' story of the lost sheep has influenced the feel and the shape of almost all the stories I have told ever since. My latest is the New Testament character Timothy telling his own life-story. This is how I begin:

What do you want to be when you grow up?
I was keen on running, and I wanted to be Olympic champion. I was never good enough, of course. But I ran and ran, and hoped and dreamed.
At all the other subjects at school, I was average to good. Except one. What's your best subject? Guess what mine was ... No – Religious Studies. Had to be, really, 'cos I'd been learning it so long. I didn't start learning the Bible when I was seven or eight. I didn't start when I

was five, which was the age we had to start learning it by law. My mum couldn't wait that long to teach me about God.

Guess how old I was when she started ... No – I was just a baby. I sucked in Mum's faith in God at the same time as I sucked her milk. As soon as I could understand anything, she told me the Old Testament story. She knew it all off by heart, and I learnt it from her.

It became part of my life. When I was about to do something I knew I shouldn't, the words of God came back into my mind: 'Don't do it, son. It isn't good for you.'

I didn't intend this, but I can see that the way I imagine Timothy is very like the little black lamb. The stories we liked as children are a powerful resource when it becomes our turn to tell them. If ever you are stuck for a story or topic, why not retell your favourite childhood story?

TELLING BIBLE STORIES TO CHILDREN

Many of the tips outlined here will fit any kind of storytelling, not just from the Bible.[2] However, I am focusing on Bible stories because they feature largely in the work we do in church children's groups. (It is just as helpful and important to tell stories set in modern life, and there are tips on that in later chapters.) Similarly, I am concentrating here on children's groups because this is where the majority of readers will be doing their storytelling. If you are going to speak at all-age services, you may need to adapt some of these tips slightly.

The tips come at three levels:

- Beginners, start here
- Growing more experienced
- So you want to be an expert!

You don't need to read all three. Choose the level that is right for you. If you are not sure, go through them until you find one that fits, then work on that.

Beginners, start here

Make the time to prepare
Don't rush it – you need time for the story to grow on you and in you.

Ask God to help you

Read the story several times in the Bible
Use the translation that the children in your group are accustomed to.

Note any words / ideas hard for children to understand
This example uses the story of Zacchaeus (Luke 19:1–10):

> Jesus was going through the city of Jericho. A man was there named Zacchaeus, who was a very important tax collector, *[see 1 below]* and he was wealthy. *[Why? Just well-paid – or a cheat? See 2.]* He wanted to see who Jesus was, but he was not able because he was too short to see above the crowd. He ran ahead to a place where Jesus would come, and he climbed a sycamore tree so he could see him. When Jesus came to that place, he looked up and said to him, 'Zacchaeus, hurry and come down! *[How did J know Z's name? See 3.]* I must stay at your house today.'
>
> Zacchaeus came down quickly and welcomed him gladly. All the people saw this and began to complain, 'Jesus is staying with a sinner!' *[See 4.]*
>
> But Zacchaeus stood and said to the Lord, 'I will give half of my possessions to the poor. And if I have cheated anyone, I will pay back four times more.' *[What made him say this? What did he mean by it? See 5.]*
>
> Jesus said to him, 'Salvation *[see 6]* has come to this house today, because this man also belongs to the family of Abraham. *[See 7.]* The Son of Man *[see 8]* came to find lost people and save them.' *[See 6.]*

Jot down how you would make these ideas/words simple, clear and up-to-date. (If you are not sure yourself, who could you ask?

If *they* are not sure, have they a commentary on Luke's Gospel that would help?) Here are my notes on the above passage:

1 Jesus' country was ruled by a foreign government which used people who lived there to collect money (taxes) to pay for roads, soldiers, etc.

2 Tax collectors had to pay a set amount to the government. Many of them charged too much and kept the extra for themselves.

3 Perhaps Jesus asked someone in the crowd. More likely, he overheard them; they were probably pointing and shouting at Zacchaeus nearly as much as they were at Jesus.

4 In God's eyes, a sinner is anyone who falls short of his laws for human living, ie all of us. But here the people were using the word to mean a real baddie: 'He sides with the enemy *and* he cheats – yerrrrgh!'

5 Meeting Jesus makes you change the way you live. Zacchaeus said, '*If* I have cheated…', but he was really owning up to it. According to Jewish law, he had to give back what he had stolen with twenty percent interest or, in some cases, a hundred percent (Lev 6:2–6; Num 5:6–7; Exod 22:2–3,7,9). 'I'll do better than that,' said Zacchaeus, already feeling generous like Jesus, 'I'll double the worst case scenario, and give back *four* times as much. Better still – I'll give half of all I own to the poor.' No law told him to do this, it was a straight 'Thank you' to Jesus.

6 Zacchaeus was rich, but he was lost. His greed for money had led him out of God's kingdom and family. Jesus came to find him and others like him, to make them friends again with God and his people. This is what 'save' and 'salvation' mean in the Bible. Zacchaeus' readiness to give his money and possessions away proves that Jesus' rescue act had worked. Jesus could only stay for a day, but salvation moves in for good.

7 All Jews are descendants of Abraham, but they are not automatically saved. They enter God's family when they start to trust and follow him as Abraham did (Gal 3:9). Jesus began by building a new Israel among the Jewish people who believed in him. He then opened the door to believers from all other countries.

8 This is a kind of nickname Jesus used for himself. He took it from an Old Testament vision of the great king God will appoint at the end of time (Dan 7:13–14). But with children, simply replace it with the name 'Jesus'.

Obviously, you won't need to say all of this as you tell the story! But it is a pool of background knowledge to help you explain any difficult bits. It will be especially helpful if you look at the Bible passage with the children after you have told them the story. They will ask about anything they don't understand.

Put brackets around any parts you think are needless detail…
…or that are not in the main action you want to tell the children. Here I would probably leave out:

- The setting in Jericho (v1)
- The detail of the tree being a *sycamore* (v4)
- Jesus' words at the end, which sound like a comment to the crowd or to his followers (vs9–10)

Now shape what's left into –

A beginning that makes people sit up and take notice
You want to grab their attention. So make it sound as if the story is going to be interesting, even exciting. Which is the better of these two openings?

> Today's story is about Zacchaeus…
> 'No, please, mister, don't turn me in. I'll get you the money by next week…'

Another way you could start is with the crowd gathering to see Jesus:

EVERYBODY was there. You'd have thought they'd won the cup. But in fact they were bursting to catch sight of just one person. Someone mega-special...

The main action of the story

This keeps moving fast. Here the action is Zacchaeus wanting to see Jesus so badly that he *runs* and shins up a tree; seeing Jesus stop right below him, look up at him and actually talk to him, even invite himself to stay the night! There's no time to describe the Jericho landscape or weather – just get on with the story!

A climax

This is the high point the story is leading up to. For me, in the Bible verses telling the story, this must be verse 8. Zacchaeus – the baddie, the cheat, the rat – is giving it all back! With interest!

Not just twice what he took. Not just three times. But, for you my darling, FOUR TIMES AS MUCH! Plus free hand-outs to the poor. Run up, run up. Christmas is early this year.

A quick ending...

...to drive home the impact of the climax without frittering it away. If you started with the crowd, you might finish with the effect of the story on them.

'That's scary,' they whispered. 'Jesus doesn't only make people better on the outside. He can get right inside you and change you there! He's turned someone we hated into someone we like. Scary – but cool.'

On the opposite page is a useful grid (adapted from a Scripture Union Training Unit module) which you may copy and use every time you are preparing to tell a Bible story. Use the boxes to note what comes in each section. This should keep you on track, saving you from getting off the point.

Break the story down into short and simple sentences

The Bible usually tells its stories in the fewest words possible, because the original writers' paper was so expensive. This led

STORY	
Bible book (chapter and verses):	
Beginning	Verses
Action	
Climax	
Ending	

them to write long, condensed sentences. For example, verse 2 of the Zacchaeus story is one sentence, but it tells us three things:

- A man was there named Zacchaeus.
- He was a very important tax collector.
- He was wealthy.

To bring the story to life for children today, give each part its own sentence, probably its own paragraph, as you fill in the detail they need to understand what's going on. But make those sentences and paragraphs short. Keep each paragraph to four sentences maximum; each sentence to twelve words; each word to three syllables!

Practise telling the story aloud ahead of time
Tell it to the furniture in your home, or to a willing friend or family member (don't worry if you feel self-conscious at first). There are three reasons for doing this:

- To give you confidence and get you used to standing up and spouting the story.
- To give you advance warning of any problems about the way you plan to tell it.
- To check that it takes about the right length of time.

Growing more experienced

On the first few occasions you tell a story to children, the steps described above will take you all your time. And you never reach a stage when you don't need to do them. But, in the same way as when you learned to walk, the steps become steadily easier, quicker and more automatic. You get to know the Bible stories better yourself, and you develop an instinct for words and ideas that will get through to children. This will leave you time and space to work on other aspects of the storyteller's art.

PREPARATION

Be clear why you are telling this story on this occasion
We don't tell Bible stories just to fill up time or do the children good in some vague way. Check with the leader, or the teaching programme you use, how the story fits in with the rest of the session. Then let that teaching theme shape how you tell the story.

For instance, the Zacchaeus story may have been chosen to illustrate the truth that Jesus finds people who are spiritually lost. In that case, I would want to retain Jesus' words in verse 10. I would probably use them as the ending, as Luke did. I might even make them the climax. I would want to start by showing what it felt like for Zacchaeus to be lost. And the action should show Jesus searching for him and finding him.

Leave out or cut down whatever doesn't fit your aim. If the point is that 'Jesus finds lost people', I may not need to mention the words 'save' or 'salvation': the aim-sentence (ie 'Jesus finds lost people') says it all in other and simpler words.

Connect the story with the children's own experience
You want them to feel that they are on familiar ground and can get inside the thoughts and feelings of the main characters. So, what are the contact points between the Zacchaeus story and what children know about today? Climbing trees? Having someone to stay

in your house? Being unpopular? Cheating? Or, if this is the teaching aim, how about an experience of getting lost?

Weave one or two of these familiar topics into the story. Perhaps especially use one of them as the beginning. Get the children busy in their memories and imaginations, so that they are right beside you in the middle of the story's action.

Connect the story with your own experience

Your life is a one-off. No one else has lived through the same mix of events, people, challenges and feelings as you. So bring your own unique mind to bear on understanding and reliving this Bible story. On this occasion, the children are going to view it from *your* standpoint and enter it through *your* senses.

I am below average height and was markedly so as a child. Oh, the humiliation of being measured back-to-back with my cousin who was the same age as me but grew ever faster! So when I hear that Zacchaeus was 'too short to see above the crowd', all my sympathy buttons start flashing. I know *exactly* how I'd have felt if I'd been him. This is an obvious entry point for *me* to tell the story. Not all the children listening will be shorties like me, but some of them will, and I can help them stand beside Zacchaeus (almost literally!). I can also help the others to understand, because that's something I really know about.

Now that my mind is focused, I can see how my experience will help with another part of the story too. Being small was a hopeless handicap at the back of a crowd, but it was brilliant for getting to the front. My family always made me buy the interval drinks in theatre bars, because I could worm my way through the crush. No one could see me or stop me because I was down near their waists! Perfect raw material for describing Zacchaeus' mad scramble to the tree.

What makes the story come alive and ring bells for you?

PRESENTATION

As you grow more comfortable with telling the story, more on top of the basic task of getting the words out in the right order, your mind has space to do other things at the same time. It can stand back and help you be aware of what's going on.

You (the storyteller) are telling *it* (the story) to *them* (the listening children). Preparation so far has focused on the story. Now think about 'you' and 'them'.

You

You are a wonderfully rich resource for telling stories. You are not a confined plastic-and-metal machine. You are a live person in contact with other live people. God has given you three vital pieces of equipment for making contact and telling stories.

Your voice

Without one of these you are at a real disadvantage! But with a voice, you can achieve a spellbinding variety of effects. If you think of yourself as a sound system, you have got four control switches you can adjust.

- **Volume (loud or soft)** – you may need to vary this to get the children's attention and keep it! Most people assume you need a loud bellow to be heard over the noise. In fact the best teachers manage to hush an unruly class by speaking more and more quietly – which probably takes lots of experience to master!

  But the volume knob is a great help in telling the story. When Jesus spoke to Zacchaeus up the tree, did he have to shout to make himself heard? As he came face to face with the most hated man in town, was there perhaps an electric silence as he issued his invitation privately in a whisper? Was the crowd's reaction a raucous outburst of protest? Or did they mutter to each other behind their hands? There are no obvious right answers. It's up to you to decide and bring out as you make the story happen in front of your listeners.

- **Pace (fast or slow)** – your voice should follow the rhythm of the action. So when you come to Zacchaeus running ahead or coming down the tree in a rush, report it quickly. When Jesus stops and looks up, slow right down. Even stop the story altogether. Stories need pauses at dramatic moments. The listeners need time to drink in the scene, to work out what's going on, to wonder what might happen next.

  It is also good to speed up or slow down at other times, when the words themselves don't force you to. Less important detail – or things the children can follow

easily – can go faster. But something harder to
understand – or close to the story's main aim – will need
more emphasis. Whatever you have decided to make the
climax of the story should probably be spoken very
slowly ... with a dramatic pause.

- **Pitch (high or low)** – again, follow the action with your
voice. Zacchaeus goes up, and then comes down. Jesus
looks up and speaks up into the tree. Later, he and
Zacchaeus talk together on the level.
    But you can also use pitch in giving the characters
different voices. You may or may not feel comfortable
about using regional accents, but you can still make
people's voices sound distinct. You may want Zacchaeus
to sound gruff and low-down like a typical baddie, or
you could make his voice thin and squeaky to convey his
height. It might then seem obvious to have a contrast by
making the crowd's words the opposite pitch to his. But
it will be more realistic if you have two or more voices
in the crowd talking to each other. You will then need to
vary *their* pitches!

- **Tone or mood** – don't worry if it sounds too difficult to
keep changing pitch. A lot of it goes automatically with
changing tone to match the mood. Try saying a friend's
name angrily – then teasingly ... then sadly ... then
sexily – and you will see what I mean. In storytelling,
start with the words that indicate the mood:

He *wanted* to see who Jesus was, but he was not able ...
[He] welcomed him *gladly.* All the people saw this and
began to *complain...*

Put those moods strongly into your voice when you
come to them. Then look at the other spoken words:

'Zacchaeus, hurry and come down!'
'I will give half of my possessions to the poor...'
'Salvation has come to this house today...'

What was each person feeling as they spoke? Well, put that emotion into the words as *you* say them.

Finally, look at any parts of the story where there must be deep feelings hidden inside the bare facts.

A man was there named Zacchaeus, who was a *very important* tax collector, and he was *wealthy*.

How did Zacchaeus feel about these facts? How did the people feel? How can you use your tone of voice to bring those feelings out as you explain those bits of information?

Your face

You have a huge advantage over audiocassettes or CD players that reel out a recorded voice. Your voice transmits out of a face, which adds a picture to every word. Seeing a story is a hundred

Look how our faces can convey some of the commonest feelings. Where might each of these come in the Zacchaeus story?

times better than just hearing it. The important thing is to make sure your face shows it clearly and well.

Watch a child's face to see how naturally expressive it is. Most of the time our faces match our words like that. But in storytelling we should increase the effect, because we need to be seen by a number of people at once and some of them may be quite a distance from us (make sure everyone can see you clearly).

When you are reporting a conversation, it may help to turn your head first one way, then the other, to show which person is speaking. With Zacchaeus, you should also have him always looking up because he is shorter than everyone else!

Your body
We are, of course, not just faces on sticks. We have arms, hands, legs, bodies – all capable of helping the story to get up off the page and walk. We don't have to be professional actors, but it is a real help if we can mime some of the action. We may not have much room to move around in: a lot will depend on how big our group is and where we meet. By and large, it is better to sit with the children than to stand over them. But even sitting, it is still possible to add gesture and movement.

Some of the Zacchaeus story cries out for actions to match the words. I would find it impossible to say, 'He was too short to see above the crowd', without standing up on tiptoe (or kneeling) and leaning this way and that to peer through a forest of imaginary heads. And I couldn't say Jesus' words, 'Hurry and come down', without at least beckoning.

There are other moments that will come alive with a thoughtful pose or gesture. Here are some possibilities:

> Zacchaeus ... was wealthy ... *[Show Zacchaeus keeping some of the tax money for himself and stuffing it into a pocket or wallet.]* ... welcomed him gladly ... *[Usher Jesus through the door with a grin on your face – and then blow a raspberry at the crowd as you shut the door in their face.]* And IF ... um ... *[embarrassed pause]* I have ... er ... cheated... *[get this word over very quickly and quietly]* anyone ... *[Clear throat, blow nose, then bite fingernails while shuffling nervously from foot to foot.]*

Over to you for more ideas:

> **Zacchaeus STOOD and said** ... *[How could you show his mood through the way he stands?]* '**I will pay back four times more.**' ... *[What gestures are needed to confirm this promise?]* '**The Son of Man came to find lost people and save them.**' *[How might Jesus have reinforced this with a movement?]*

Of course, there is no rule that says you can *only* use your voice, face and body to tell a story. Use any other prop or visual aid if it helps. It can sometimes be effective to have a set of large faces like the ones on p20, and to show each at the right moment in the story. Or you could make them into masks to cover your face.

With Zacchaeus, the obvious object to help you bring the story to life would be some money, whether coins or notes, real or artificial. This way you could show the proportion he kept for himself and the hoards he took to the bank or hid under his bed. You could show him counting out half for the poor and fourfold pay-backs for those he had cheated. Or if you (or a friend) are good at drawing or making gadgets, you could show him working out the sums on a giant calculator or computer.

Winnings ÷ 2 – (4 x what I cheated) < Salvation!

Just beware of any gimmicks hijacking the story and burying the original aim. Keep them as visual *aids*, not show-stealers.

Them

You aren't telling the story to an empty room. You have a living, lively audience who will join in the story, given half a chance. And better even than hearing and seeing a story is to become part of it themselves. To tell a story really well, you need audience participation. This opens up the real power of storytelling: it helps people get inside the original event – not just to learn about it but to feel it. At the same time, it helps you check that the children are following the story and understanding it.

To begin with, as you build up confidence, you might want just to get them to repeat key words:

Zacchaeus kept saying, 'I WANT TO SEE JESUS' ... When he heard Jesus was coming to his town, he said, 'I WANT TO SEE JESUS' ... He didn't think he should leave his tax office, but then he said, 'I WANT TO SEE JESUS' ... There were two very tall people in front of him, so he said, 'Excuse me, but I WANT TO SEE JESUS' ... Then he thought, 'It's no good staying here, because I WANT TO SEE JESUS'...

Then, at the end, you could get them to learn Jesus' closing words (v10) and say them with you. Or you could ask them questions at various stages:

Have any of you ever been lost?
What would you have done if you couldn't see?
What does it mean to call someone a sinner?
What do you think he did next?

When you are sure you can keep control of the children, get them to be the crowd. You don't have to make them get up and move around (unless or until you want that). Just cue them in, sitting where they are, when you want them to say something. Ask them what the crowd thought about Jesus. What sort of things were the people saying as they waited and watched? What did they think about Zacchaeus? What did they say when he turned up? You could get the children to say what they suggest each time you mention the name 'Zacchaeus'. What *other* names (other than 'sinner') did they call him behind his back? (Careful!) What did they think and say when Zacchaeus made his 'reformed character' speech?

Then, if you want to, you can gently let the children in on the action. You might let several of them in turn try to see over or through or round a wall of taller ones. If you have the space, let 'Zacchaeus' race the others to the nearest tree. You could hand money back to the people who have been cheated – *very* popular if you've got chocolate coins. But plan your timing carefully: don't do something fatally disruptive until after the climax of the story, or make it the climax if appropriate (but keep your sense of mischief in check!).

So you want to be an expert!

If you work on the above tips for the beginner and growing stages, you will make a good workmanlike job of telling Bible stories to children. But if you are likely to be doing it regularly for months, even years, ahead, there is yet more to learn.

Here are my top tips for tip-top storytelling which I've picked up from experts.

Take the time and trouble to develop your skill

You should be regularly doing at least some of the exercises in the 'Things to do' section (pp27–29).

Pray for love

When you love God, and you love the story, and you love the children you are telling it to, they will know it. The vibes will be exactly right. They will hear Jesus' love ringing through your words and his words as you recount them. They will know the story is not just about something that happened long ago, but about a God who is here with us now.

Learn ways round the cry, 'We've heard it before'

Find an unusual angle that will keep the children guessing for a bit. Could you try telling the Zacchaeus story as if *you* were one of the crowd (ideally a child)? Or another tax collector? Or Zacchaeus himself? Or even Jesus? Imagine the whole story happening to you as that person.

Help the children to like the central character

They must care about the hero and want things to turn out well for him / her. If you follow the Bible in making Zacchaeus himself the central character of this story, you mustn't make him too nasty: there must be something loveable about him. Help the children see what they have got in common with him. So don't make him a monster: make him an ordinary person with a problem to conquer, a fault he needs to grow out of, a wound that needs to be healed. But think carefully whether Zacchaeus should be the central character or hero. Perhaps you would do better with one of Zacchaeus' victims. They would obviously start by hating Zacchaeus and longing for justice, but how would they react when

Jesus befriends him and even stands up for him?

Perhaps the hero should really be Jesus. If so, you certainly need to be an expert storyteller! You will have to get beyond the 'stainless white robe' image and explore the thoughts and feelings Jesus may have had. What did he want and hope for Zacchaeus? What were the obstacles he had to get over? How did the crowd's reactions affect him?

Whoever you choose to make the hero, look at the background info through that person's eyes. Don't just explain the Roman tax-collecting system in general: show how it worked for Zacchaeus, or Jesus, or whoever is the main character. This way, you will help your hearers to identify with him.

Major on action and conversation

Use them even where the Bible gives straight information. It says, 'Zacchaeus was a very important tax collector, and he was wealthy.' But it will be more interesting for us to see him in the office bossing all the junior tax collectors around. Then to go back home with him in the evening and watch him showing off his luxury items.

For conversation, you don't have to have two or more people talking. It's just as good to hear one person thinking aloud. Perhaps this could be Zacchaeus' own reactions to his lifestyle, and why he wants to see Jesus.

Learn to do without notes

The essence of good storytelling is to have the story fully planted in your mind. You shouldn't need any paper or book in your hand. This will set your hands (and whole body) free to bring the story to life.

This is doubly important if you have a large audience to control. Expert storytellers can use their hands to direct the audience rather like the conductor of an orchestra. They switch the mood from suspense to gloom or glory with a flick of the wrists. A beckoning motion, and people are on their feet to line the roadside; a flat palm, and they are sitting again; a finger to the lips, and all is quiet.

Even more important, your eyes are free to look at the listeners and meet their eyes. This eye contact sets up a contract with the audience, in which you trust them to respond to your lead. At the lowest level, it lets any disrupters know you are watching them. But more positively, eye contact is at the heart of all good communication. When you don't look someone in the eye, you are holding yourself back from them. But when you 'see eye to eye', you are building a relationship with each hearer. It helps them feel you are giving the story to them personally.

Some people rely on their knowledge of the story to carry them through, calling the words to mind at the time. Others work hard on the exact words and order of events as they prepare: they may need to learn their version of the story by heart. Not everyone can manage this, but it's good if those who can, do. It is the same as actors learning their lines in a play.

Go beyond seeing the story as an end in itself

God is wanting to do something with it in the lives of its hearers, and you can help him. This 'life application' may be part of the teaching aim:

> The story of Zacchaeus shows that (1) Jesus wants to find and save lost people; so (2) we can turn to him when we feel lost.

Ideally, your telling of the story should work on (2) as well as (1). You will then be helping the children to know that the same Jesus who became Zacchaeus' friend then, wants to be our friend now.

Much better than tacking on a sort of 'moral' at the end is to weave it as a continual strand throughout the story:

> Can you think of anyone today who might feel a bit like Zacchaeus did?
> What do you think Jesus wants us to do if we have cheated anyone?
> What do you think Zacchaeus said to Jesus next after the end of the story?
> What would you like to say to Jesus now?

Develop your own style as a storyteller

By the time you have mastered all the tips in this chapter, your way of telling stories will be quite different from mine. It really will be your own way, and not by the book.

Some people get the children to act the story out in full. Their input is then a constant dialogue with the 'listeners' who are, of course, doing much more than just listening. Others find they are good at telling stories with puppets, cartoons or a stock character from television (Zacchaeus meets Postman Pat or Oprah Winfrey). What might your speciality be? If you have an idea gestating inside you, give it a try.

• Things to do

These ideas are graded at three levels – 'Beginners', 'Growing more experienced' and 'Experts'. Choose the level that is right for you. The activities are a mix of practising your skills, learning from your successes and mistakes, and learning from others. Some you can do on your own, some would be better done in a group (eg the team who lead the children's work in your church).

BEGINNERS
• Ask someone whose opinion you respect to make comments on your efforts.

• Ask someone more experienced – perhaps your team leader – to help you prepare the next Bible story you tell.

• What was your favourite Bible story as a child? If you are friends with some children, or have got some of your own, tell it to them in your own words. Try to recapture what was so special about it.

• Practise telling a story you know well to a person you know well, who doesn't make you feel embarrassed. Ask them to tell you:

What they enjoy about the way you tell it.
Anything they don't understand.
Anything they think might work better if you tell it another way.

• Go back to Jesus' story of the lost sheep (Luke 15:1–7) and / or his teaching about the good shepherd (John

10:7–15). Try preparing your own children's or all-age story based on one of them, working through the steps for Beginners (pp11–16).

GROWING MORE EXPERIENCED
- Once you have told a story, don't throw it away or forget it. Review it. Ask yourself:

  How far did I achieve the aim?
  How well did I get the main point across?
  When and how did I lose their interest or attention?
  What should I learn from this to improve my storytelling?
  What should I remember to do (or not do) next time?

- Listen to a tape of children's bedtime stories, or watch Scripture Union's video retellings of Bible stories (eg Roy Castle in *Mark Time* or Philip Sherlock in *Joseph*). Which parts do they do well? What could you learn from them? What could you try in the next children's story you tell?

- Take a closer look at the two stories at the beginning of this chapter – the little black lamb and the one about Timothy's childhood. How far do they live up to or fall short of the chapter's tips for telling stories to children? Are they faithful to their Bible bases (Luke 15:3–7; 2 Tim 1:5; 3:14–17) or do they distort them? How would you advise the stories' writers to improve them?

- Take five Bible stories that are often told to children. Work out what you think was the point the original teller or writer was using each story to teach, and write it in a sentence. Or, if you think there are several points, choose one that would make a good teaching aim for children.

- (This exercise is for 'Experts' too.) Take another of Jesus' parables (eg the lost coin, Luke 15:8–10), or another of his dealings with people (eg Mary of Bethany, Mark 14:3–9; John 12:1–8). Think how you would tell the story to a children's group or at an all-age service.

Work on one of the tips in 'Growing more experienced' or 'So you want to be an expert!' (pp16–27).

EXPERTS

- Listen to yourself on tape or watch yourself on video. Don't do this until you are reasonably experienced and confident – it can be shattering at first! This is partly because we don't see or hear ourselves as others do. But once you have got over the shock, you will notice mannerisms in your speech and gestures that need ironing out. Also – more positively – effective moments to repeat and develop. Check whether your tone of voice is lively or monotonous. Make sure it isn't patronising! Is your face's neutral mode friendly and smiling or an off-putting frown? (Some people may tell you to practise in front of a mirror. This may work for them but I find it too distracting to be any use.)

- Watch other storytellers – at church, on television, or just good raconteurs in everyday conversation – to see what makes them good. What can you adapt for yourself?

- Read other books on storytelling.

• Quotes

Children's imaginative growth depends on stories as much as their physical growth depends on vitamins and proteins. Stories extend the child's vision, deepen his understanding, exercise the emotions.

Survey report in The Listener, April 1975

There is no greater resource for children than the stories of the Bible. Bible stories express the human condition and probe man's inner problems, yet explore them with a hope offered by their testimony to God, who speaks through them to young and old.

Larry Richards, Talkable Bible Stories, Baker Book House (US)

GO OUT AND GET THEM

'Paulette will ring you,' they said at the book shop. 'She needs to talk to you before you get to the church on Sunday.'

I had been asked to tell stories to the children at a Sunday service in Worthing but it seemed there was some slight difficulty. Paulette would sort it out.

'Can you come early?' she asked. 'You see, we have to go out and collect the children before the service starts.'

???

She explained ... 'When I took over the 7–8 year olds here, I asked God what he wanted me to do. He said, "Go out and get them." Our church has been seeded into a run-down housing estate. There are a lot of problems, but the children really know how to pray. They call themselves a Bible Study Group, and that's what they are.

'I buy your books and lend them out to the children. They all know your name and want to hear you talk, but we have to call at the houses to get them to come.'

I thought, 'This is not me, Lord!' But I arrived at the church early and was bustled out by Paulette. We turned left into a housing estate and started knocking on doors. Kids spurted out. It was rather like the Pied Piper. Knock, knock, look who's here, yes, it really is her, Veronica Heley's come specially to tell you stories, so are you coming this morning?

One boy left his FOOTBALL GAME to join us!

Trailing kids, we returned to the church where the walls were bouncing in and out with praise songs. After a short time we followed Paulette out into the street, turned right and into the front room of one of the houses on the estate. Most of the furniture had been removed so that we could pile in. Thirty-two kids, Paulette and I crammed into that room, sitting in layers on the floor. We left the door open so that some teenage hangers-on could hear from the hall.

If anyone wanted to scratch their leg, they had to get their neighbour to lift his / her arm first.

It was great. I told stories, and it seemed at times as if they were holding their breath, so as not to miss a word. Then we lifted the roof with a chorus and went home tired but contented.

Veronica Heley, Candle and Keyboard, August 1994,
The Fellowship of Christian Writers and Watson, Little Limited

• Resources

DIAL A BIBLE STORY

'Hi Kids!' has existed in other parts of Europe for several years and is now available in the UK. It provides five-minute Bible-based stories for children on the telephone. Each week there is a new story communicating a Christian message through a real-life situation.

Most homes have a telephone, and children feel important having their own number to ring. The child chooses the timing of the call and is therefore most receptive at that particular moment.

At the end of each story, children are invited to write or telephone to become members of the 'Hi Kids!' club for 6–12s. Membership includes a newsletter with information about local activities for children.

For further information, contact **Hi Kids!, PO Box 13100, London W14 9FL; tel/fax 0171 386 8638.**

• Notes

1   Abridged from *The Little Black Lamb* by Marjorie Procter, Blandford Press, an imprint of Cassell plc, 1983 reprint of earlier edition.

2   I have tried to base these tips on my own experience, but I am also passing on wisdom that has helped me – from *Know How to Tell a Story* by Clifford Warne; *Seven Plus* by Margaret Old; *Working with Children*, The Upside Down Trust's Do-It-Yourself Training Pack; *The Adventure Begins* by Terry Clutterham; and notes from training sessions led by Elizabeth Barratt and Brenda Rogerson.

2 Stories for teenagers

In the name of the Father, the Son and the Holy Spirit.
Amen.

Every preacher began this way and it was the signal to switch off.
My secondary school was a church foundation, and our assembly
each day took place in the chapel. Once a week we had a longer
service with – boring beyond belief – a sermon. It was the deputy
head today. He wasn't quite as deadly as some of them. Perhaps
I'd allow him an open ear for half a sentence.[1]

> It was the night before the coronation and the young
> King was alone in his chamber. The lad, being but sixteen
> years of age, fell asleep. And as he slept he dreamed a
> dream…

Hello, what's this? Not quite the usual 'My text today is taken
from the book of…' This sounded – well – *interesting*!

> He thought he was in a long, low attic, amidst the whir
> and clatter of looms. Pale, sickly-looking children were
> crouched on the huge crossbeams. Their faces were
> pinched with famine, and their thin hands shook and
> trembled. A horrible odour filled the place. The air was
> foul and heavy, and the walls dripped and streamed with
> damp.

'Psst!' My neighbour Mark nudged me. 'Look at Stinky.'
Our chemistry teacher, sitting at the end of the row, was gap-
ing at the deputy head in disbelief. Such an unconventional
approach obviously bordered on the scandalous for him.

The young King went over to one of the weavers, and stood by him. And the weaver looked at him angrily and said, 'Why art thou watching me? Art thou a spy set on us by our master?'

'Who is thy master?' asked the young King.

'Our master!' cried the weaver, bitterly. 'He is a man like myself. Indeed, there is but this difference between us – he wears fine clothes while I go in rags, and while I am weak from hunger he suffers not a little from over-feeding. But what are these things to thee? Thou art not one of us. Thy face is too happy.' And he turned away scowling, and threw the shuttle across the loom, and the young King saw it was threaded with a thread of gold.

And a great terror seized upon him, and he said to the weaver, 'What robe is this that thou art weaving?'

'It is the robe for the coronation of the young King.'

And the young King gave a loud cry and woke...

I was hooked. I didn't discover until years later that the story was by Oscar Wilde. But I could sense the quality. The 'olde worlde' language was no barrier: it told me we were in a time long past and added to the atmosphere.

The chamberlain and the high officers of state came in and made obeisance to him, and the pages brought him the robe of tissued gold, and set the crown and the sceptre before him.

And the young King looked at them, and they were beautiful. But he remembered his dream, and said: 'Take these things away, for I will not wear them.'

And the chamberlain said: 'How shall the people know that thou art a king, if thou hast not a king's raiment?'

And the young King plucked a spray of wild briar that was climbing over the balcony, and bent it, and made a circlet of it, and set it on his own head. And thus attired he passed out of his chamber into the great hall, where the nobles were waiting for him.

And the nobles made merry, and some of them cried out to him, 'My lord, the people wait for their king, and thou showest them a beggar', and others were wroth and said, 'He brings shame upon our state, and is unworthy to be our master.' But he answered them not a word, but passed on, and went down the bright porphyry staircase, and out through the gates of bronze, and mounted upon his horse, and rode towards the cathedral...

Hey, this is *good*. I suppose he'll stop and give us a lecture in a minute. Hope not, though. I'd rather stick with the story.

The old bishop went to meet him, and said, 'My son, with what crown shall I crown thee, and what sceptre shall I place in thy hand?'

And suddenly a wild tumult came from the street outside, and in entered the nobles with drawn swords and nodding plumes, and shields of polished steel. 'Where is this king, who is apparelled like a beggar?' they cried. 'This boy who brings shame upon our state? Surely we will slay him, for he is unworthy to rule over us.'

And the young King bowed his head, and prayed, and when he had finished his prayer he rose up, and turning round he looked at them sadly.

And lo! through the painted windows came the sunlight streaming upon him, and the sunbeams wove round him a tissued robe that was fairer than the robe that had been fashioned for his pleasure.

He stood there in a king's raiment, and the Glory of God filled the place, and the saints in their carven niches seemed to move. And the people fell upon their knees in awe, and the nobles sheathed their swords and did homage, and the bishop's face grew pale, and his hands trembled. 'A greater than I hath crowned thee', he cried, and he knelt before him.

And the young King came down from the high altar, and passed home through the midst of the people. But no man dared look upon his face, for it was like the face of an angel.

Wow! Now for the moral, I suppose.

In the name of the Father...

We stumbled to our feet. What, no moral? It's over and I didn't want it to finish! That's a first. And I heard every word – a double first!

I must have sat through nearly two hundred sermons in that place, but that's the only one I can remember. Partly because it was different. But largely, I think, because it was a story. Stories weave their own magic and hold you captive. You don't want to escape because you just have to know how it will end. Even if you're a cool, self-conscious teenager. Of course, the last thing you want is to be treated like a child. If I'd sensed it was a childish story, if he had used a formula like 'Once upon a time', even if he had started by saying he was going to tell us a story – my hackles would have been up. But he got through to my human, ageless love of stories before I knew what he was doing. Everyone agrees that *children* love stories. But it isn't only children – we *all* love stories, as long as the wrapper is acceptable.

I think there is another reason why that story made a big impression on me then and has stayed with me ever since. Its meaning wasn't obvious – it was subtle, partly hidden. Why was the deputy head telling it to us in chapel? He must have seen a Christian 'message' in it, but what? Was it about Jesus? Or just about true nobility in general? As I listened I wasn't getting everything handed to me on a plate. I had to work to understand it. And once you start working at a story, it can work on you. You won't just remember it – it becomes part of you. At one level or another it becomes *your* story. For me, Wilde's 'The Young King' is like a life-improving virus: it got under my skin and I can't shake it off.

• TEACHING YOUNG PEOPLE

I should have remembered these lessons when I in turn became a teacher. But I didn't – I had to learn them again.

While I was a college student, I helped each Easter and summer on a Scripture Union holiday for boys. The main teaching method was short talks morning and evening, where we spelt out different aspects of how to become a Christian or how to live as one. This was a perfectly natural arrangement to me because I was used to similar sermons on Sundays and academic lectures on weekdays.

But when I started teaching in a school where most of the students were not committed Christians, I realised this wouldn't do. If you tried a straightforward talk or sermon about being a Christian they switched off, just as I had done as a teenager. I came to see that in the holidays we were ladling spoonfuls of Christian doctrine into people who were willing to receive it. But at school I needed to use indirect communication, or 'oblique' communication as I called it at the time. As I saw it, there were at least five reasons for this.

Professional

I was employed as a Religious Studies teacher, not an evangelist. It was appropriate to explain what Christians believe, even what I, as a Christian, believe; but not appropriate to tell my students what they should believe. That would savour of indoctrination. I tried always to be honest about what other beliefs or viewpoints were possible, while reminding people that I didn't hold them myself!

Cultural

I (and, I guess, many of my generation) didn't want to be paternalistic, as many of our rather frightening teachers had been. I didn't see myself as some remote dispenser of knowledge, beyond interruption or contradiction. I wanted to be a friend, to get alongside my students and learn with them in some directions as much as they would learn from me in others.

Educational

It was fashionable at the time not to lecture our students with endless facts but, as far as possible, to help them discover facts for themselves by research and observation, and to form their own opinions. To me this is not just a modern fad but a sound educational principle, as in the ancient Chinese proverb:

I hear – and I forget.
I see – and I remember.
I do – and I understand.

It's inhuman to expect people just to sit and listen and be told everything. God has made us inquisitive creatures who like (and need) to make discoveries for ourselves.

Psychological / 'developmental'

People in their teens are no longer at the stage of simply accepting what authority figures say. They are emerging adults themselves. They need to prepare for independence. They have to build up the ability and the confidence to fly the nest. So it is quite right for them to check everything out. They naturally treat the older generation, especially teachers, with a healthy dose of scepticism.

Spiritual

Another piece of ancient wisdom, this one in the Bible, says, 'Whoever is stubborn after being corrected many times will suddenly be hurt beyond cure' (Prov 29:1). Not everyone responds positively to the good news about God. Some reject him, and the more they hear of him the firmer their rejection becomes. If we go on and on about Jesus to them, we end up doing the very opposite of what we want. We actually stiffen their resistance, making them less receptive and more likely to run into God's final judgement without asking for forgiveness. This led me to a study of the teaching methods Jesus used.

• THE WAY JESUS TAUGHT

How did Jesus get through to people? In particular, did he have different approaches for those who were ready to accept his message and those who weren't? There seemed to be two quite distinct audiences in the Gospels:

- His followers or disciples who were to some degree committed to him.
- The crowds who were far less so.

• The committed / Jesus' followers

I looked at John chapters 13–16, Jesus' last supper with his closest followers and friends. This is a concentrated teaching session, but more like a seminar or practical workshop than a half-hour sermon. It starts with a bit of action (Jesus washing the disciples' feet) and, according to Matthew, Mark and Luke, later includes more action (when he teaches them to remember him with bread and wine). Jesus asks them questions or prompts their reactions. At the same time they are free to interrupt him with any questions that occur to them on the spot. When they don't understand they ask him to make it clearer, or when they feel too awkward to express their confusion they mutter to each other until Jesus gets the message.

I studied the whole of Mark's Gospel and found exactly the same picture: whenever Jesus taught the disciples he used question-and-answer discussions (Mark 8:14–21,27–33; 9:9–13, 30–50; 10:23–45; 11:12–14,20–25; 14:17–31), he replied to their questions and observations (4:10–20; 7:17–23; 10:10–12; 12:41–44), or he gave practical instructions for their own mission work (6:7–13; 10:13–16). The only time Mark records him giving anything remotely like a continuous lecture is his teaching about the future in chapter 13 – but even that is in response to the disciples' questions (13:3–4) and, as there were only four of them present at the time, it seems unbelievable to me that they sat politely silent for twenty minutes while Jesus held forth. Small groups of friends aren't like that! It's just that on this occasion Mark hasn't recorded their follow-up questions and interruptions.

So at our school Christian fellowship I didn't give a talk as I would when I visited other schools to speak. I led a Bible study, where we looked at a Bible story together and discussed it. Any questions or comments were allowed as long as they genuinely had something to do with what the Bible was saying or with what it means to live for God today.

• The less committed / the crowds

When it came to teaching the crowds, Jesus often used dialogue and discussion (Mark 2:15 – 3:6,23–35; 7:1–16; 10:1–9,17–22; 11:15–18,27 – 12:40), but he also made big use of the teaching tool he is most famous for – parables. He used them even more, apparently, with the crowd than with his disciples: 'Jesus used stories to tell all these things to the people; he always used stories to teach them' (Matt 13:34). Actually, not all his parables were stories (the word 'parable' just means 'comparison') but most of them were. And they are, quite simply, the most brilliant stories ever told. A friend of mine once introduced a writing workshop with the words, 'Jesus' story of the lost son is the most famous short story in the world – unless it's the good Samaritan by the same author.'

But why did Jesus tell parables? Not, of course, in order to win the Nobel Prize for Literature. Chapter 4 of Mark's Gospel records a whole set of Jesus' parables, and it suggests two main reasons why he used them. At first sight, these reasons seem to contradict each other. The 'obvious' one, the one most people would think of straightaway, is that he told parables to make his teaching clear:

> Then Jesus said, 'How can I show you what the kingdom
> of God is like? What story can I use to explain it? The
> kingdom of God is like a mustard seed, the smallest seed
> you plant in the ground. But when planted, this seed
> grows and becomes the largest of all garden plants. It
> produces large branches, and the wild birds can make
> nests in its shade.'
> Jesus used many stories like these to teach the crowd
> God's message – as much as they could understand.
>
> *Mark 4:30–33*

The story, or comparison, seems perfectly simple. God's kingdom – ie the number of people who follow Jesus in obeying God as their king – started very small. It was just Jesus and his disciples. But, he said, it would grow steadily until it was so big it would reach into other countries and include foreigners and outsiders. This is bracing, fortifying truth, but Jesus didn't announce it in direct language. He put it in picture language and made it visual. And he put it in story form, which made it memorable. You only need to hear the story once and you've got it. You could repeat it, almost word for word, to someone else.

But, at the same time, Jesus also cloaked the truth. He put it into code language and hid it. Someone not on the inside and in the know might well miss the point. This is exactly what Jesus gave as his other reason for telling parables:

> Later, when Jesus was alone, the twelve apostles and
> others around him asked him about the stories.
> Jesus said, 'You can know the secret about the king-
> dom of God. But to other people I tell everything by
> using stories so that:
> "They will look and look, but they will not learn.

They will listen and listen, but they will not understand." '

Mark 4:10–12

It sounds weird. Is Jesus saying he tells parables to *stop* people understanding? Well, in a way, yes. He isn't saying he *wants* to confuse people and shut them out. But this will be the effect of his teaching on some people. His 'look and look, listen and listen' words are a quote from Isaiah (Isa 6:9–10). God warned his prophet then that the people he was speaking to were spiritually blind and deaf. They would hear his words with their physical ears, but they would not accept his message. Jesus understood that it would be the same for him with most of the people he spoke to. His parables work at two levels: those who are self-satisfied and unresponsive hear only the surface story; but the spiritually hungry crack open the outer casing and find inside the kernel of what God is getting at.

John records an example of this happening when Jesus drove the money-changers out of the temple.

The Jews said to Jesus, 'Show us a miracle to prove you have the right to do these things.'

Jesus answered them, 'Destroy this temple, and I will build it again in three days.'

The Jews answered, 'It took forty-six years to build this Temple! Do you really believe you can build it again in three days?'

(But the temple Jesus meant was his body. After Jesus was raised from the dead, his followers remembered that Jesus had said this. Then they believed the Scripture and the words Jesus had said.)

John 2:18–22

Jesus planted his parable like a seed in the ground. The Jews took him literally, and it confirmed their view that he was mad. But in the good soil of his disciples the story lay dormant until, in due season, it came to life and bore fruit.

Often, of course, the meaning was obvious enough to anyone with eyes to see – or Jesus pointed it out. He didn't leave his questioner to form his own conclusions about the parable of the rich fool, he pushed home the story's challenge: 'This is how it will be for those who store up things for themselves and are not rich towards God' (Luke 12:21). And what about the devastating fire-power of the parable of the vineyard? This is clearly a skirmish in the struggle between Jesus and the Jewish leaders.

> A man planted a vineyard. He put a wall around it and dug a hole for a winepress and built a tower. Then he leased the land to some farmers and left for a trip. When it was time for the grapes to be picked, he sent a servant to the farmers to get his share of the grapes. But the farmers grabbed the servant and beat him and sent him away empty-handed. Then the man sent another servant. They hit him on the head and showed no respect for him. So the man sent another servant, whom they killed. The man sent many other servants; the farmers beat some of them and killed others.
>
> The man had one person left to send, his son whom he loved. He sent him last of all, saying, 'They will respect my son.'
>
> But the farmers said to each other, 'This son will inherit the vineyard. If we kill him, it will be ours.' So they took the son, killed him and threw him out of the vineyard.
>
> So what will the owner of the vineyard do? He will come and kill those farmers and will give the vineyard to other farmers.
>
> *Mark 12:1–9*

There is no doubt who or what Jesus was getting at:

> The Jewish leaders knew that the story was about them. They wanted to find a way to arrest Jesus, but they were afraid of the people. So the leaders left him and went away.
>
> *Mark 12:12*

I guess that most of Jesus' parables were in fact part of the conflict. The story of the lost son, for instance, is not some timeless moral fable: it is part of Jesus' retort to the Pharisees' attack on him. The elder brother represents them, the younger brother the tax collectors and sinners who were flocking to hear Jesus (Luke 15:1–2,11–32).

This picture of the parable as a spiritual weapon – a sort of time-bomb – gripped me. I was in enemy territory. Most of the boys in the school were not committed Christians. And part of their spiritual blindness was to think they knew it all already. After all, we studied Mark's Gospel for O Level (yes, this really was the prehistoric days before GCSE). So when it came to my turn to take assembly, I could see that a direct assault would turn them off. But if I could slip through their defences with something indirect, something a bit niggling and teasing – well, perhaps I could plant it in their minds and memories. God might then work on it later and bring some of them to faith.

I came up with a story loosely based on Jesus' parable of the rich fool (Luke 12:16–21).[2] I think this is an ideal parable to use with teenagers: it challenges materialistic attitudes with a really gutsy story. But today I would use a version like this one by Anita Haigh. It follows the rap rhythm of Hale & Pace in 'The Management':[3]

Listen to this story Jesus told about a FOOL
Who, 'cos he had a lot of dosh, thought he was dead
    COOL.
He owned a hundred acres of large and fertile fields
And with his R-reg tractor PLANTING CROPS WAS
    NO BIG DEAL.

But he had a dilemma – his barns were far too SMALL
And his harvest was a bumper one – where would he
    keep it ALL?
'I know what I will do,' he said, 'I'll tear my old ones down
And build the biggest-ever barn, THE ENVY OF THE
    TOWN!

'All the windows I put in will be UPVC
And I'll fit an anti-theft device for more SECURITY.
I'll put my name in neon lights to show who owns the lot
And there I'll stash away my crops AND EVERYTHING
    I'VE GOT!'

And feeling very satisfied he poured a glass to TOAST
Himself for all that he had done – 'I've got a right to
  BOAST!
For all my great achievements, I raise this glass of sherry
And now I'll take life easy – I'LL EAT, DRINK AND BE
  MERRY!'

But then he heard the voice of God – 'You fool, do you
  not KNOW
This night you'll die and then, my friend, where will your
  riches GO?
And all these things that you hold dear, in which you've
  placed your trust
Will then be taken from you AND LEFT TO ROT AND
  RUST!'

So the moral of this story is plain for all to SEE,
That worldly riches cannot give a lasting GUARANTEE.
A man's true life is not made up of things he might own,
But everlasting treasure IS FOUND WITH GOD ALONE.

TELLING PARABLES

There are two main possibilities with parables:

• Retelling Jesus' stories.
• Creating new parables of our own.

Retelling Jesus' parables

It's not enough to repeat the story as it stands. You need to recreate its impact in the modern world of the listeners. In her rap about
the Rich Fool, Anita did this by taking a popular modern storytelling style, well-known from television. Retelling one of Jesus'
stories set among the world and the characters of *The X Files* or
Red Dwarf would be another good approach. But sometimes the
problem is more subtle. The name 'Samaritan', for instance, has
none of the meaning for young people in Britain today that it had
for Jesus' countrymen in his time. In fact, Jesus' story has been so
powerful that it has waved a magic wand over the word
'Samaritan' and transformed it: it now means someone who cares

for depressed people and saves them from suicide. Back then it meant the enemy. Riding Lights' popular sketch, 'The Parable of the Good Punk Rocker', is a good, funny attempt to catch the feeling of disgust Jesus' listeners would have felt towards Samaritans.[4] But it was more tense and racial than that. I once tried telling it as the parable of the good IRA man. However, I was safely in England at the time. You would only really feel the risk and courage of the story if you told it to a strongly Unionist gathering in Northern Ireland. There it would cause an explosion. You would either be lynched, or – as Jesus meant – the story would unleash a flood of love strong enough to conquer the problems.

The other difficulty is the sheer fame of Jesus' stories. Everybody knows what's going to happen, so the ending has none of the shock value it had when he first told it. Whatever substitute you choose for the Samaritan, your whole audience knows he'll be the goodie. The only way to get back to the knock-down effect of the story is actually to turn it inside out. In the 1970s, the Kairos Group tried this with their version of the story:[5]

> Soon a priest passed the spot where the man lay; but he was too afraid to stop for he knew the dangers of the road well, and besides he was on his way to Jerusalem to do his duty in the temple. So he hurried past knowing that it was more important to reach Jerusalem, than to stop and look at a man who was probably dead anyway. But he did think to himself, 'Somebody should do something about it.'
>
> Soon afterwards a Levite passed by, but he was afraid as well and he too had an important meeting to attend in Jerusalem … Just like the priest, he too thought, 'Somebody should do something about it.'
>
> Not many minutes later a Samaritan reached the spot. He was afraid as well, and as he led his ass along behind him, he saw the man lying by the side of the road. He was naked and bleeding, and although the Samaritans and the Jews hated each other, the Samaritan felt sorry for the man; but he also had an important meeting to attend, and as he looked with compassion at the man lying there, he said aloud, 'Somebody really should do something.' And as he spoke – the man died.

This version punches us in the solar plexus when we are looking the other way. It makes us shout out, 'No, you've got it wrong!' And that means this version has got it right. It has managed to open us up at last to what Jesus is saying. We can't leave it to the good old Samaritan. The somebody who should do something is – us.

Creating your own parables

This is another way of getting round the 'We know what's going to happen' syndrome. One good source is the illustrations you hear in sermons. They are often flashes of inspiration or mini-stories that you can work up into something longer and stronger. At one stage I kept hearing the illustration that Christians should be like the Sea of Galilee and not the Dead Sea. The Dead Sea takes water in but gives none out, so it is stagnant and nothing can live in it. Galilee, on the other hand, is a freshwater lake: the Jordan flows into it, but also out again at the far end. From the days of Simon Peter until now, it has been full of fish. So, to be spiritually alive, Christians need to give out as well as take in. Great, I thought, and developed it into my 'Parable of the ponds'. It is the life-story of a rain-drop falling into the Stream called Servis, flowing through Lake Luvving, but finally drying up in Dead-End Ditch.

However, there is a difference between a parable and an illustration. Preachers use illustrations to clarify the point they are making. It's like the coloured wrapper they throw away once they have got to the point inside. But a parable is its own point and its own illustration. It is the contents as well as the wrapper. It is itself a vehicle for the truth, not just a sidelight on the truth. You don't want to throw it away but leave it to go on working. So be careful about moving on to explain a parable or apply it. Jesus seldom explained his parables, and then only to his inner circle when they asked him (Matt 13:10,36). Usually, he left the story hanging with just the briefest conclusion: 'You people who can hear me, listen' or 'Which one of these three men do you think was a neighbour? ... Then go and do what he did' (Matt 13:9; Luke 10:36–37). Ideally, build clues into your parable so that it will do its own explaining and instructing inside anyone motivated enough to go on thinking about it.

Another source of parables is the world around us. Jesus told stories about seeds and trees as well as the more usual kings and merchants. This is no surprise: the God we worship is the God who made the world. His workmanship is full of patterns and rhythms for us to learn from. When I became a Christian, I tried to explain to my sceptical friends what had happened. I often felt stuck for words, but one day I came across this lovely parable by John White.[6] It uses a parallel in the animal kingdom to express what I was trying to say. I have often used it with sixth-formers and students.

Powerful thrusts from his vigorous legs propelled the frog to Bubu's side. He was a new member of the Little Pond Philosophical Society and Bubu greeted him warmly. Though the frog appeared to Bubu to be bound by superstition, he nevertheless showed promise.

'Beautiful day,' said Bubu.

'Beautiful,' agreed the frog. 'And up above it's tremendous. I never knew such colours existed before my conversion.'

If Bubu was embarrassed, he gave no sign of it. 'I don't doubt your sincerity in the least,' he murmured smilingly, 'though I suspect that your conversion is merely a psychological phenomenon.'

'You mean that my legs are in some way unreal?' the frog asked.

Bubu was at home now. 'Not at all. I would say that your legs are the real result of your faith in something unreal. I noticed that you began to develop them about the same time you started talking about your fantastic 'world' of 'air' and 'sunlight' and 'insects'. For myself, I prefer to be intellectually honest. I refuse to exploit the cheap benefits that come from living in a world of fantasy. I cannot sacrifice my integrity and believe in what I know to be untrue, even if by doing so I could gain a pair of legs.'

The tiny tadpole's dignity seemed pitiful, as he quivered beside the frog's vigorous young body. Pity filled the frog's eyes.

'But, Bubu,' he said quietly. 'The world up above that I talk about *is* real. I can't explain it, but in a sense it's more real than the watery universe we live in.'

'More real *to you*.'

'More real to anybody, Bubu.'

'But not at all real to *me*.'

'Bubu, the world would be there whether I could feel it or not. Right now, as we talk, soft breezes blow across the surface of Little Pond. Other frogs like me are leaping across dry ground. Bubu, I've seen clouds, I've been warmed by the sun, I...'

The tadpole's annoyance nearly choked him. 'Show me!' he cried. 'Show me this sun. Show me a piece of dry.'

'I have to admit,' the frog said, 'that it's impossible for me to show you the sun. If you are to see it, your eyes will have to change. There's a verse in the Sacred Book that says, 'Unless a tadpole metamorphoses, it cannot see the kingdom of dryness.' I hope one day to take you hopping with me between blades of grass. But if I took you right now, just as you are, you'd die. You couldn't stand the exposure.'

The frog stretched his legs uneasily. 'It's so stuffy down here,' he said. 'I have to go up for a gulp of air more frequently these days. So if you'll excuse me...'

The frog darted away, thrusting powerfully upward through sunbeam curtains toward the surface of a world that did not exist...

Inspired by this, I also came up with a story of a caterpillar turning into a butterfly, which I often use in schools.

Ordinary stories work too

Parables have a lot to offer, but don't get hung up on them. Straight stories can also work well. Back on the SU holiday, I resolved never to give a straight talk again but to convey the teaching through stories. They seemed so much more entertaining and enjoyable than solid doctrine. When other inspiration failed, I told stories about a fictional schoolboy and the 'wise old doctor'. At college, I'd lived in a flat next door to a Christian doctor who included the local boarding school in his practice. He even had some of the boys living in his house, and it was thrilling to watch him build up a pastoral ministry alongside his medical duties. In those days there was a series of 'Jungle Doctor' books for children, so I told 'School Doctor' stories – inspired by my neighbour – to teenagers! And I discovered, in the New Testament itself, the patron saint of all bored teenagers – Eutychus, who fell into a deep sleep as Paul 'kept on talking until midnight' (Acts 20:7–12)! My own version, called 'Boring Sermons', was the story I told more than any other in those years working with young people.

My current story for young people continues the autobiography of Timothy introduced in chapter one. In this scene we see an event from The Acts of the Apostles through the eyes of Paul's young assistant. My research suggests he was about eighteen at the time.[7]

…I could feel a shiver of joy tingling down my spine. My first time away from home – 500 miles away – but God was still with me. I just knew it! You could almost see Paul planting the Bible words I was reading into people's minds as they listened.

But at that moment the spell shattered. There was this blood-curdling, unnatural voice from up the road: 'Look! There they are!'

'Oh, not her again!' I groaned. 'That's every day this week.'

This wild-eyed slave-girl ran towards us. 'These men are servants of the Most High God,' she shrieked at everyone standing by. 'They are telling you how you can be saved!'

She was a fortune-teller; people hung on every word she said. At first we thought her free publicity would do us good. But now we realised she was blocking God's work, taking our audience away every time we began to get through to them. She had an evil spirit in her who was abusing her.

Well, this was one time too many for Paul. He stopped preaching and spoke to the spirit: 'In the name of Jesus Christ, I order you to come out of her!'

Everyone went stock still – it was like everything was in slow motion. The girl seemed to get smaller and

smaller, like a shrivelled balloon. Suddenly she looked —
just ordinary. I realised she was just a frightened young
girl the same age as me.

'What have you done to her?' shouted her master.
'You've taken away her powers.' He came up to Paul,
snarling in his face.'You can't do this, you know. That's
our livelihood.'

The crowd was growing all the time, and he turned
to them for support:'Here! Help me take them to the
magistrates.'

Several men closed in on Paul and Silas and hustled
them up the street to the market-place. The crowd
swirled behind them. I sat very still and found myself all
alone. That felt the safest place to be, and it was the
hardest thing I'd ever done to force myself up and follow
the others — a short way behind.

When we got to the square, there were two Roman
magistrates hearing cases.'What's this about?' they
asked.

I wormed my way through the crowd and saw the
girl's master looking all sly. 'These men are Jews, causing
trouble in our city. They're teaching us to break the law.'

I couldn't believe it. It was all lies. We'd only been
telling people about Jesus, nothing about breaking any
laws. But the crowd started rumbling and I didn't like
the sound of it:'Jewish scum! Jewish scum!'

I thought at least the magistrates would make it a
proper trial, with witnesses and evidence. But they just
turned to the big guards behind them and pointed at
Paul and Silas. Two guards came down and grabbed Paul,
another two took Silas. They ripped their shirts off and
roped them to some posts beside the platform.

'You can't do this,' I quavered. 'They're Roman citi-
zens.' I wanted to shout out loud. I wanted to say I was
one of them too. But I just couldn't.

The guards picked up birch sticks from the platform.
They took turns to run and swipe Paul and Silas's bare
backs. I felt quite sick as I watched. Nasty red stripes
appeared on Paul's back, then blood, then — worse.

I lost count of the strokes before I turned and ran…

• Things to do

The following exercises are extra to the basic training and practice given in chapter one. Continue to work on any suggestions from that chapter that you find helpful and relevant.

- What stories appealed to you as a teenager? What could you learn from them that would help you teach the faith to young people today?

- What TV programmes do the young people in your church watch? What comics do they read? How could you put Bible stories and the gospel in the same idiom and style?

- Study Jesus' teaching methods for yourself. Either use the passages listed on p39, or look at one of the other Gospels. What strikes you as important for the way we teach young people today?

- Try retelling one of Jesus' parables, or creating one of your own. Follow the tips outlined on pp44–50.

- Think of a young person in the Bible who the teenagers you work with might relate to. How could you present the story to them – telling it aloud, or perhaps through a Bible study? Prepare something ready to use.

• Quotes

Tell all the truth, but tell it slant...

Emily Dickinson

A parable is one of those stories in the Bible which sounds at first like a pleasant yarn, but keeps something up its sleeve which suddenly pops up and knocks you flat.

P G Wodehouse, quoted in The Parables Then and Now by A M Hunter, SCM, 1971, p10

A MENTAL HAND-GRENADE

The official head of the Protestants in Lebanon was, until his recent death, the Rev Ibrahim Dagher. In the autumn of 1967 a theological college in Lebanon where I was teaching was requested by its Board to conduct a series of public lectures relating to the war in June. We did so. The last of the series was led by three Middle Eastern pastors. Each spoke in turn. The first two gave a strong, fair, rational appeal for support of the Palestinian cause. They spoke for some forty-five minutes. Lastly, Rev Dagher, a Lebanese nationalist, rose to his feet. He spoke as follows:

'Once there was a bedouin who had a camel. On a cold night the camel said to the bedouin, "My nose is very cold. May I put my nose in your tent?" The bedouin said, "Tafaddal" (Please go ahead). A bit later the camel said, "My ears are very cold. May I put my ears in your tent?" The bedouin said, "Tafaddal." Then the camel said, "My neck is still in the cold wind. May I put my neck in your tent?" The bedouin said, "Tafaddal." The neck of the camel is very strong. When the camel had his neck in the tent, he jerked his powerful neck upwards and struck the top of the tent with his head, and the tent collapsed on the bedouin and on the camel.'

Rev Dagher then sat down. That was eighteen years ago. The present text is, to my knowledge, the first time that this parable has ever been recorded on paper. The audience instinctively recognised that the camel symbolized the Palestinians, the bedouin referred to the Lebanese and the tent represented Lebanon. The point of view expressed is that of the Lebanese nationalists. My purpose here is not to agree or disagree with Rev Dagher's views, but rather to examine his methodology. The conceptual content of the parable is straightforward. He was saying, 'We the Lebanese have welcomed our Palestinian brothers into Lebanon, but there is danger lest they break down the social and political structures of Lebanon and bring the whole country crashing down around our ears.' The climate in which we lived in 1967 would not have allowed such a public statement.

But, he did not say anything! He just told a 'simple'(?) story. A number of analytical observations can be made.

First, an old familiar story was retold but with some critical revisions. Everyone in the audience thought they knew how the story was going to end. They assumed that in the end the camel would drive the bedouin out of the tent. The revisions in the traditional story went off like a mental hand-grenade and Rev Dagher's main point was located in those revisions. Second, the author of the parable gave what his fellow Lebanese deemed a 'wise answer' and thereby gave the community a good feeling about the rightness of following this particular leader. Third, the lecture hall was electrified and the parable was rendered quite unforgettable to all those present irrespective of their views. I venture to suggest that I have recorded above at least 80 per cent of Rev Dagher's 'ipsissima verba' even though I heard the parable once eighteen years ago. All of this happened in the modern sophisticated city of Beirut, not in a small rural village, yet the parable survived in Protestant circles and was retold all across the Middle East. Indeed, in the summer of 1984 the parable was repeated to me intact in Bristol, England, by a witness who had heard it in Jordan in the late sixties.

Kenneth E Bailey, 'Informal controlled oral tradition
and the Synoptic Gospels', reprinted in Themelios 20/2, 1995

• Notes

1 Abridged from 'The Young King' by Oscar Wilde.

2 My parable 'John' is printed in *Drama for all the Family*, Kingsway, 1993, pp161–162.

3 Anita Haigh, *Rap, Rhyme and Reason*, Scripture Union, 1996, pp22–23.

4 Paul Burbridge and Murray Watts, *The Best Time to Act*, Hodder and Stoughton, 1995, pp57–59.

5 The Kairos Group, *Jesus is Alive*, Falcon, 1972, pp95–96.

6 Abridged from 'Metamorphosis' in John White, *The Race*, Inter-Varsity Press, 1984, pp95–101.

7 Adapted from my book, *In the Steps of Timothy*, Inter-Varsity Press, 1995, pp54–55.

3 Stories for sermons

James had a new book with him this morning. Not a word in it. Not yet. Every page was fresh and clean. The old one, you see, was filled up and took its place on the shelf. What would be the first topic, the first words, to adorn page one of the new hardback in his coat pocket?

For James was on his way to church. Like one or two others in the congregation, he was an avid, almost obsessive note-taker – and he had a sneaking suspicion that this set him apart from some of the rest, like that short-sighted older man, the mother with her three children, and the newcomer who seemed, let's face it, virtually illiterate.

Came the hymn before the sermon, the prayer, up spoke the preacher, and out came James' new book, his Parker pen at the ready...

Twenty minutes later, it was still there. The empty book, that is – and the pen now folded inside it. Nothing like this had ever happened before. Whatever was going on?

The preacher started like this: 'Charlie had never been to Africa before. And as he lay there in the grass, scared out of his mind and dripping with sweat from both heat and fear, he vowed that if he ever got out of this alive, he'd never go again. The man with the gun had surely seen him...'

And so it went on. Of course, James had heard sermons like this before, starting with a gripping drama and then, after ten minutes, switching to 1 Kings chapter 9. But this one was different. For one thing, the story went on, and on. It didn't lead *into* the sermon: it seemed

to *be* the sermon. For another, James had no idea how
the story ended.

So his nice new book, and pen, were soon forgotten.
Like the man, and the mum, and the newcomer, James'
eyes and ears were riveted – not so much on the
preacher but on the grass where Charlie lay, on the man
with the gun and on that sound coming from the track
on the far side of the trees...[1]

• STORIES FOR ADULTS?

All my adult life I have been a regular speaker in adult church services. But I have no stirring memories of hearing a great story sermon. The story above is, sadly, fiction. I had to start telling stories
to adults gradually, painstakingly, on my own. Stories were taking
over my attempts to teach the faith to young people. And I asked,
'Why not adults too?'

I still ask this question. After all, Jesus preached in stories to
adults, not just teenagers. Much preaching in adult services today
seems to me to miss its mark, because it ignores the overwhelm-
ing case for using stories in this context as well. Some adults think
they should be fed 'solid truth' rather than 'mere stories', but
they've got it wrong.

• Stories are popular

WE ALL NEED STORIES SOME OF THE TIME

The way God made our minds means we can't exist on a diet of
nothing but facts and reasoned arguments. The left side of the
brain deals with these, as it functions logically step-by-step.[2] But
the right side of the brain works more with feelings, instinct, intuition. It needs input that treats life whole rather than broken into
components, history not science, stories not information. On this
line of reasoning alone, to meet the needs of the human mind half
our sermons should be in story form.

SOME OF US NEED STORIES MORE OF THE TIME

Most sermons seem designed to appeal to that intellectual, left
side of the brain. Perhaps this is because most preachers are 'left-
brain' people, that is, brought up and trained to control their thinking with the rational side of their brains. But at least half

(probably more) of their listeners are 'right-brain people': in their brains the more spontaneous, creative right side dominates. They find left-brain sermons hard work, even boring. They warm to something more colourful and stirring. Stories bring them to life and get them involved.

MOST PEOPLE LIKE STORIES MOST OF THE TIME

These were the ten most popular television programmes for the last 'normal' week of 1996, before the Christmas-New Year schedules took over.

1 *EastEnders*
2 *Coronation Street*
3 *Heartbeat*
4 *Emmerdale*
5 *Casualty*
6 *The National Lottery Live*
7 *Neighbours*
8 *The Thin Blue Line*
9 *The Bill*
10 *Only Fools and Horses*

All stories – except the Lottery, and even it has spawned a stream of stories about winners and what becomes of them!

Surely we should learn from this if we want to pass on God's message to the human race. OK, so we're trying to educate people, not merely entertain them. But that doesn't mean our teaching sessions have to be like an Open University programme. Why shouldn't they have something of a TV soap's drawing power? Churches can't muster the resources of our television stations, but we have a script full of stories just as lively and exciting as theirs. And of course, God's stories are far more important. They tell us about the Creator who made us and will judge us. They show us what he is like and what we are like. They explain what's wrong with the world and what God has done to put it right. They should appeal to a mass audience.

WE ALL TELL STORIES ALL THE TIME

Some left-brain people, trained to preach scholarly sermons, think they are no good at storytelling. But even if they aren't telly addicts, they are in fact absorbing and telling stories the whole time. They may not realise this if they think 'stories' have to be made up or rewritten from history. But stories can also be real life and happening to us now. My day is jam-packed with stories, and I guess I'm quite typical. I get up and turn on the radio to hear the news – the latest stories from around the country and the world. I read the Bible and then newsletters to help me pray for my friends. At work my assistant tells me how she is. When my children get back from school, they watch *Neighbours*; my wife and I betray our age by listening to *The Archers*. As we eat we share the jokes and hurts, the triumphs and disasters of the day. Some evenings we meet a group from church and catch up with what's happening in each other's lives. Back home I return some phone calls and exchange news. At last I relax with a video and then a read before falling asleep – a novel, a biography, my sports magazine. It's stories, stories, stories from dawn to dark. Stories aren't a strange language just for children or arty types: we hear and tell them all day. They should be a natural form for our preaching to take.

• Stories are good at the job

STORIES ENGAGE MORE OF THE PERSONALITY

A lecture appeals to the mind and sometimes the will, but stories appeal to our emotions as well: they touch our hearts. A sermon can spell out the lessons God taught Moses or David, but a story can recapture the wonder and scariness of following him across a desert. The reason is simple: stories fit the whole of us, life-size, in a way that other forms of speech don't. Human life comes story-shaped. We are all making our own story as we journey through life and, like a TV soap, our lives happen in daily episodes. The natural way to learn from the Bible is to put its story alongside ours, to compare character with character, experience with experience, lesson with lesson.

STORIES MAKE US THINK

You might suppose that an interesting lecture would be the best way to make people think. But, in fact, we think when we are moved, and the way to move people is to tell stories. Take Samson, for example. The writer of Judges presents him to us as an early Arnold Schwarzenegger.[3] This story is exciting, funny, alarming, disturbing. And because it moves us in these ways, it also moves us to think. Has Samson gone too far? Will God desert him? Can God really use such a flawed character? How can he let someone like that lead his people? The writer doesn't answer these questions. He doesn't even ask them, in so many words. He simply tells the story. But because it's a powerful story, it stirs up the questions in us.

STORIES GIVE LISTENERS THE SAFE SPACE THEY NEED

This is part of the magic of stories. They draw listeners in and get them involved. But to do so, they need to start by allowing listeners to keep their distance. The clearest example of this in the Bible is in the story told by Nathan. God sends him to condemn David for seducing Uriah's wife Bathsheba and then having Uriah killed. How does he set about it? 'Thus says the Lord: you have sinned…'? No, not at first – that approach puts the defences up. Instead, he tells a story:

> 'There were two men in a city. One was rich, but the other was poor…'

This is safe territory for David. It's not attacking him personally. It invites him to listen in.

> 'The rich man had many sheep and cattle. But the poor man had nothing except one little female lamb he had bought. The poor man fed the lamb, and it grew up with him and his children. It shared his food and drank from his cup and slept in his arms. The lamb was like a daughter to him.'

Aaaaaahh! It is artfully, brilliantly done. David, like all of us, is hooked. He is totally won over to the poor man's side.

> 'Then a traveller stopped to visit the rich man. The rich man wanted to feed the traveller, but he didn't want to take one of his own sheep or cattle. Instead, he took the lamb from the poor man and cooked it for his visitor.'
> David became very angry at the rich man…

Done it! David's feelings have become so involved in the story, he joins in. He can't stop himself pronouncing judgement.

> He said to Nathan, 'As surely as the Lord lives, the man who did this should die! He must pay for the lamb four times for doing such a thing. He had no mercy!'

And so David has walked out of his safe space into the firing line. He has just sentenced *himself* to death.

> Then Nathan said to David, 'You are the man!'
>
> 2 Samuel 12:1–7

Stories create their own world, and you think you are watching it from the outside. This is partly why adults enjoy the talks in all-age services and learn so much from them. We think they're for the children, and so it's safe to listen. We drop our guard, we get involved – and suddenly God is speaking about us and *our* world.

Stories do a brilliant job. They are the most effective form of human communication ever devised. So why aren't more of our sermons stories? But we still haven't reached the strongest reason why they should be – which is…

• God loves stories too

LOOK HOW MUCH OF THE BIBLE IS IN STORY FORM

Twenty-two of the sixty-six books are narrative, telling the history of God's people. This may sound like only one-third of the whole. But they tend to be longer than the purely teaching or preaching books – Genesis is longer than Joel, Matthew than Romans, and so on. On a page-count, it is 644 pages of narrative against 587 pages of proclamation or instruction. Of course, some of the story books, like the Gospels and Acts, include sermons; but at the same time there are narrative sections in what are basically books of sermons, like Isaiah and Jeremiah. Some books of solid instruction or argument, such as Deuteronomy and Job, are set in the story of how they were first spoken. And the visions in Revelation are not abstract paintings, but scenes and events in story form. So if we are to reflect the Bible's balance in how we teach the faith to adults, it should be at least as much storytelling as explaining theological ideas or laying down moral rules. At least as much – or, I would say, even more. The case gets even stronger when we allow for the next fact.

Even the non-story parts are part of THE story

It's not that the story parts of the Bible are little nuggets of narrative in a book of rules or wise sayings. It's exactly the other way round. Moses delivered his laws, Solomon his proverbs and Amos his prophecies as part of the story of Israel. The whole Bible is the story of God and his world, from the moment he created it to when he will recreate it new. Each book of the Bible fits somewhere into this story.

This means that even the non-story parts have a story behind them. It helps bring them back to life and give them extra meaning for us. For example, it is impossible to read the letter to Philemon without bumping into the story of Onesimus, the runaway but converted slave – he is what the letter is about. And we can only hear Paul's letters to Timothy clearly when we know who Timothy was, what he was meant to be doing when Paul wrote, and what had happened to make Paul say what he did. Once we hear the words speaking into their original story, we can work out more clearly what God wants us to learn from them today. In the same way, several of the psalms have headings telling us when they were written. Psalm 51 is headed 'A psalm of David when the prophet Nathan came to David after David's sin with Bathsheba'. We don't know for sure if these headings are original and reliable, but there is no strong reason to doubt them. And what colour and depth they add if true. The words of Psalm 51 are clearly suitable for someone turning their back on adultery and murder.

> Create in me a pure heart, God,
>   and make my spirit right again…
> God, save me from the guilt of murder,
>   God of my salvation,
>   and I will sing about your goodness.
>
> *Psalm 51:10,14*

If David could seek and find forgiveness after such blatant wrongdoing, nobody is too bad to enter God's kingdom. We've got good news for the whole world – and even words they can use as a response to it.

But there is even more of a clincher...

NEW TESTAMENT SERMONS ARE THEMSELVES STORIES

Peter and Paul didn't present the good news about Jesus as a set of four spiritual laws or three steps to take towards God. They told Jesus' story! On the Day of Pentecost, the heart of Peter's message was:

> 'Jesus from Nazareth was a very special man. God clearly showed this to you by the miracles, wonders, and signs he did through Jesus. You all know this, because it happened right here among you. Jesus was given to you, and with the help of those who don't know the law, you put him to death by nailing him to a cross. But this was God's plan which he made long ago; he knew all this would happen. God raised Jesus from the dead and set him free from the pain of death, because death could not hold him...
>
> 'Jesus was lifted up to heaven and is now at God's right side. The Father has given the Holy Spirit to Jesus as he promised. So Jesus has poured out that Spirit, and this is what you now see and hear...'
>
> Acts 2:22–24,33

Paul's message was very similar. The only real difference was that he was speaking to people away from Jerusalem, who hadn't seen the events for themselves.

> 'Those who live in Jerusalem and their leaders did not realise that Jesus was the Saviour ... They could not find any real reason for Jesus to be put to death, but they asked Pilate to have him killed. When they had done to him all that the Scriptures had said, they took him down from the cross and laid him in a tomb. But God raised him up from the dead!'
>
> Acts 13:27–30

In other words, the good news isn't a set of ideas to agree to: it's a story that brings a new Lord into our lives – the story of Jesus.

Indeed, the word 'gospel' (old English for 'good news' or, more exactly, 'good tale or story'!) is the name we give to the books that record the stories about him. It should be impossible to preach the gospel without telling stories of Jesus.

Of course, Peter and Paul press home the challenge and urge their hearers to respond:

> 'Change your hearts and lives and be baptised, each one of you, in the name of Jesus Christ for the forgiveness of your sins.'
>
> Acts 2:38

> 'Brothers, understand what we are telling you: You can have forgiveness of your sins through Jesus.'
>
> Acts 13:38

But 'response' is precisely what these tail-pieces are: how to reply to the good news offered in the story of Jesus.

Underlying all this is the basic reason...

GOD MAKES HIMSELF KNOWN THROUGH THE STORY

I suppose God could reveal himself to us through a cosmic TV screen or a person-to-person phone call on our eighteenth birthday. In fact, he does so through the Bible's story of Israel and Jesus. It is a striking witness to the fact that he has designed us on his own pattern. For how do we introduce ourselves and tell people who we are? 'Hello, I'm Lance. I write books for Scripture Union. At the moment I'm writing one about storytelling...' We tell them our story. And God does the same. This is why stories about God do more than just 'tell a story'. They convey his presence. The same Jesus who loved and taught and healed in first-century Palestine is with us now. As the stories tell us the sort of person he was and is, we grow to love and trust him.

It is equally striking that the two ceremonies Jesus told us to use in building his kingdom both tell stories. When we meet, he said, we are to take bread and wine, which act out his death – his body and blood given for our benefit. And when people become Christians, we are to dip them in water, which again tells its own tale: they go down and then come up, just as Jesus died and rose again.

But remembering these past events does more than simply

remind us that they happened. The word 'remember' has a stronger meaning than that. Just as 'dis-member' means to pull a body to pieces, 're-member' means to put it together again. Retelling the story re-creates the experience. It puts us in living touch with God. When I am baptised it shows the old me dying with Jesus; a new me emerges to live with and for him. When I feed on the Lord's supper, he fills me with his life and strength. As with all God's stories, we don't just hear it; we enter it. We are part of his family, and so our stories are part of his.

• SERMONS OR STORIES?

All this raises a serious question about the way we do our preaching today. Almost always the sermon centres round the truth(s) the preacher deduces from a Bible passage rather than the passage itself. The sermon's structure is a series of points, but the Bible passage, as often as not, is a story. Why did the writers of the Old Testament record historical events, and why did Jesus tell stories if God really wants us to learn a set of doctrines or action points instead? Shouldn't they have written sermons rather than stories?

Of course, many preachers will say, 'I use lots of stories in my sermons. I'm a great believer in illustrations.' But that isn't quite what I mean. The term 'illustration' is highly revealing. It clearly implies that the important part is the point we are trying to make. The story is its servant, throwing light on it; the story is a small part of the whole. But with Jesus the story *is* the whole. He trusts the story to give us God's message without having to explain it. This takes us back to the difference we started to look at in chapter two, between parables and illustrations. Jesus' parables are not just bedtime stories to send people to sleep. He had a teaching point in mind, and he often hammered that point home at the end of the story. But the main body of his teaching was the story itself:

LUKE 18:9–14

Teaching point
Jesus told this story to some people who thought they were very good and looked down on everyone else.

Story
'A Pharisee and a tax collector both went to the Temple

to pray. The Pharisee stood alone and prayed, "God, I thank you that I am not like other people who steal, cheat, or take part in adultery, or even like this tax collector. I give up eating twice a week, and I give one-tenth of everything I get!"

'The tax collector, standing at a distance, would not even look up to heaven. But he beat on his chest because he was so sad. He said, "God, have mercy on me, a sinner." I tell you, when this man went home, he was right with God, but the Pharisee was not.'

Punch-line
'All who make themselves great will be made humble, but all who make themselves humble will be made great.'

The punch-line is the servant: it draws out what the story has made clear, and applies it to everyone.

So what about a change of approach when we are preaching on story passages? At the very least, it would be good to reverse the usual balance, which tends to make us emphasise our teaching points and carve out parts of the story to illustrate them. Instead, we should put our energies and emphasis into teaching the story itself, following its shape and outline; only then should we draw out the story's conclusions.

But better still, when we can do it, is to turn our whole sermon into a story. Follow the Bible's own structure. If it adds a moral or epilogue at the end, you can follow suit. But where it leaves the story to do its work without comment, I dare you to do the same. You may find it takes a monumental effort to keep your mouth shut. But there will be a great gain: people will have to work out the meaning for themselves instead of leaving you to dole it out to them.

Help, danger! Suppose they get it wrong!

But who's to say you always get it right when you, the preacher, work out the application for them? Don't they know their own lives and needs better than you do? And haven't they got access to the Holy Spirit to help them understand just as much as you have? Well then, give them the chance to try.

DESIGNING STORY SERMONS

There are many different forms story sermons might take:

You could tell the Bible story in your own words

Your instinct, brought up on years of sermons, might say the story on its own isn't enough. But if it was enough for Moses, or Nehemiah, or Jesus – why not for us? Who knows, your listeners might be provoked to go on meditating on the story long afterwards. Isn't that what we want?

The story I'm telling most often at the moment – Timothy's autobiography – ends by asking what happened after Paul summoned him to Rome:[4]

I walked with Luke and Mark beside Paul, past miles of tombs to where his own was going to be. Terrible place but we weren't depressed. It was strange, but we felt excited, even joyful; because really Paul was walking through the tunnel to the winner's rostrum.

'There is waiting for me the victory prize,' he kept telling us. 'The prize which the Lord, the righteous Judge, will give me.'

We sang the hymn Paul had quoted in his letter to me:

If we have died with him,
   we shall also live with him.
If we continue to endure,
   we shall also rule with him.

Then we arrived. Paul wrapped his arms round each of us and blessed us. I was last, and he held onto me longest.

'My dear, dear son, the Lord be with your spirit.'

I could find no words for an answer, just tears and a tighter hold. At last Paul said, 'The Lord will rescue me from all evil and take me safely into his heavenly kingdom.'

He slipped away from me, knelt in front of the man with the sword – and was gone.

I stared at the two empty husks – head and body – which only a moment ago had been so full of Jesus.

More of Paul's words came back to me: 'But the Lord
stayed with me and gave me strength...' I took Luke and
Mark by the arm, and said the words out loud: '...so that
I was able to proclaim the full message for all the
Gentiles to hear.'
'That means me, you know,' I said.
And Luke answered, 'It means us as well.'

You could retell a Bible story in a modern setting
Jesus' story of the Pharisee and the tax collector is a juicy candi-
date for this. As chapter two showed about parables in general,
you will need to reverse the roles to get back to the point. In modern Christian folklore, Pharisees are bad and tax collectors are
good, so the story as it stands is predictable and dull. When Jesus
told it, they were the other way round and the story was shock,
horror, scandal. A thief goes home in the right with God!

You could make a story of your own...
...to reflect the same aspect of God but in a different way. How
else does God turn our prejudices, our values, upside down? (In
the area of materialism and wealth, perhaps?)

You could use other people's stories
These can be modern or ancient. Following someone else's lead,
I have built an evangelistic presentation around the story of the
Frog Prince. Its origins are lost in the mists of time, but it makes
a wonderful parable of the Christian good news. The devil wants
to keep us trapped as deformed versions of what we're meant to
be, but a royal kiss can make us truly royal again... The Gospels
show us Jesus giving God's kiss of acceptance to everyone willing to receive it.

You could use modern or past church history
When I was a student, stories were emerging of how Christians
were being imprisoned and even tortured for their faith in East
European countries. I was so moved that, instead of preaching, I
sometimes read a chapter from their books. This can probably
only work if you are a vivid reader and have practised the reading
enough to look up and hold people's eyes most of the time. But
people made comments like 'Better than any sermon' and 'I really

felt I was there'. So much so that one person said she couldn't sleep afterwards. When did a sermon last do that for you?!

You could create a fictional character...

...(or a set of them) who tries to apply the story to his / her own life today. I once had to preach on work and leisure. So I created two typical church couples and looked through their eyes at the tensions in Mark 6:31–37: Jesus wants, on the one hand, to give us space to eat and rest; but on the other, he wants to teach us to serve other people. At the start of the story, neither couple had the balance right: one couple spent all their spare time in leisure pursuits, the other in church work. Both had to learn from the other. This approach works just as well with non-narrative parts of the Bible. Take one of the ten commandments. Tell the story of someone trying to live it out, and you have helped your hearers move from the law engraved in stone to obeying it themselves in daily life.

You could take a slice of your own experience...

...perhaps your own struggle to accept or understand part of Christian teaching, or to make it work out in practice. Let me give a special plug for telling your own story like this. I was brought up in a generation that thought it big-headed to talk about yourself. And, of course, it's quite wrong if our motive is, in Jesus' words, to 'make ourselves great'. But it's altogether different if we offer our experience to help and encourage others. Time and again, people have thanked me for being honest about difficulties I've had in learning to follow Jesus. They can see I'm an ordinary, faulty human being like them. And, I hope and pray, they can see that God goes on loving and trying to help even an awkward cuss like me. It's a way of demonstrating and teaching how to be a Christian in daily life.

It's especially helpful with controversial issues. Laying down the law will make some people disagree with you and feel they have got to oppose you. But you will disarm them if you take the line – 'This is an area where Christians take different views. I don't know for sure who's right, and I respect people on all sides. I used to think X. But then I wondered about Y. And now I'm closest to Z because ... But I'm trying to stay open to God changing my mind again as I pray about it.'

Your own story models the way we change and develop in our

understanding of God's ways. It gives your hearers permission to hold their own views with dignity, but also the space to stand back and look at them with a self-critical eye.

Short and...

Some of these approaches may leave you with something rather shorter than the traditional sermon – especially when you first try them. If this is likely to be a problem, start by using the story as one section only of a sermon. But with nerve and practice, you will reach the point where you feel able to tell the story and then stop. If it is five minutes shorter (or fifteen!) than the usual sermon, people will bless you for it. Not because they are basically lazy, but because when our words are lively and few we provoke them to think and leave them space to do it.

And space to talk about what we've said. Stories naturally lead into conversation. They are better at doing this than the average sermon – for several reasons:

• Stories are easier to follow and hear the whole of!

• They allow you to observe and form your own opinion; whereas sermons tend to tell you what to think.

• They include different people with different points of view and set up a conversation between them, so they give a pattern for the conversation to follow; whereas sermons give a pattern of one person speaking to a silent audience, and are a hard act to follow.

In this way, stories help create an atmosphere where faith can grow, as the New Testament expects:

> I know that you have all the knowledge you need and that you are able to teach each other.
>
> *Romans 15:14*

> Use all wisdom to teach and instruct each other...
>
> *Colossians 3:16*

Encourage each other and give each other strength, just
as you are doing now...

We ask you, brothers and sisters, to warn those who
do not work. Encourage the people who are afraid. Help
those who are weak.

I Thessalonians 5:11,14

Christian teaching should be interactive, involving everyone; not
a one-way monologue from the 'expert'!

• Things to do

The following exercises are extra to the basic training and practice given in chapter one. Continue to work on any of those suggestions that would be helpful and relevant.

* Reflect on an average day in your life. How much time is
  given to hearing or telling stories? How far do you let
  them be part of any Christian teaching you do?

* Reflect on your own TV diet, or that of your church
  members. What does it suggest about 'natural' ways to
  communicate? How far do your sermons or other
  teaching sessions use these?

* Look again at the two Bible stories featured in this
  chapter: Nathan and David (2 Sam 12:1–25), and the
  Pharisee and the tax collector (Luke 18:9–14). What can
  they teach you as a preacher and storyteller? Could you
  write a modern version of one of them and use it in a
  sermon / teaching session?

* How could you retell Jesus' story of the big banquet
  (Luke 14:16–24) in an evangelistic setting today? Try
  writing a modern version. Focus on the reactions of both
  sets of people, those who get to the party and those who
  miss out. Think of the likely reactions of people listening
  who are not Christians, and include them in the story.
  Then write three or four questions for people to discuss
  after they have heard the story.

- In your next sermon or teaching session, try to increase the story content you usually have, for example:

  Make the outline and headings follow the Bible story's structure.
  Make one of the illustrations a story.
  Make one of your story illustrations more self-contained, without a lengthy explanation.
  Make one of the points or sections a story.
  Monitor very carefully its effect on you and your listeners. What do you learn from it?

- Try out my suggestion that at least half our sermons should be stories. Over the next three months, either give half of each sermon you preach over to stories; or turn half the number of sermons you preach wholly into stories.

- Plan a preaching series based on narrative passages of the Bible. Don't preach sermons about the passages, but tell stories which follow or echo the Bible narrative. To vary the diet, take a different one of the tips (pp 66–69) each time.

• Quotes

To be a Christian is not principally to obey certain commandments or rules, but to learn to grow into the story of Jesus as the form of God's kingdom. We express this by saying we must learn to be disciples; only as such can we understand why at the centre of creation is a cross and resurrection.

Stanley Hauerwas, The Peaceable Kingdom,
University of Notre Dame Press, 1983, p30

Perhaps it is only in the world of fairy tales – a world we have all inhabited at one time or another, a world full of darkness, danger, and ambiguity, a world where things are not what they seem as marvellous transformations take place, a world that evokes new adventures and new possibilities, a world where good finally wins the day in a triumph of marvellous surprise – that the wonder and surprise and ambiguity and transforming power and final triumph of the gospel of Jesus Christ can be set forth.

Preachers have the highest and holiest of all fairy tales to tell ... a tale that is (incredibly!) true.

Reprinted from Telling the Story by Richard Jensen, pp114–115, copyright © 1980 Augsburg Publishing House. Used by permission of Augsburg Fortress

I've given a good deal of thought to the difference in impact between reading about slavery and watching a powerful story [on TV] (*Roots*). A book about slavery gives me all the data and facts and information that I need. *Roots* moved me ... Why can't preaching be more like *Roots* in its power and impact and less like a cold, unemotional book? ... Most of our preaching, didactic in character, imparts all of the information, data and facts. But no-one is moved. Very few go off shouting, 'I'm free! I'm free!' Couldn't we learn to tell stories in such a way that people's lives would be changed?

Richard Jensen, Telling the Story, p119

Bible stories are snapshots of God at work. Whichever story we explore, we find God doing something important in his eternal plan to save. We see him at work through the history of Israel and the rest of the world, shaping his fickle, fallible people. Perhaps most obviously, we discover his influence on and through the life of one or more individuals in spite of their failings. As we see him creatively and lovingly at work on all these levels, we shall recognise him more easily at work in our own lives, and be filled with the hope that he will work in them even more.

Terry Clutterham, The Adventure Begins, Scripture Union/CPAS, 1996, p119

• Notes

1 My thanks to Chris Idle for writing this story and letting me include it here. Chris says he isn't a natural storyteller and that he scribbled it off the cuff. Well, all I can say is, I hope I'm there the next time he preaches like this!

2 However, I think we should do our 'left-brain' teaching in churches through discussion-style seminars, not sermons (see pp69–70).

3 Or, for the more intellectual, like a Greek tragedy. This was the form the poet Milton chose for rewriting the story in his *Samson Agonistes*.

4 The story makes much use of 2 Timothy 4:9–21, and is adapted from *In the Steps of Timothy*, Inter-Varsity Press, 1995, pp195–196.

4 Stories in groups

All my adult life, on and off, I have been a Bible-study group-leader. Many training sessions and ideas have helped me, but nothing so dramatically as this printed outline for studying the story of Zacchaeus.[1]

INVITATION TO CHANGE

1 Turning points
On a sheet of paper draw a straight line. This represents your 'life-line'. Above the line jot down distinctive periods in your life, eg first school, teens, etc. Below the line jot down the place where you were living during these periods.

Now pinpoint 3 or 4 'turning points' in your life, eg 'When I took up the guitar', 'When my girlfriend / boyfriend / parents separated'. Mark them in by a line across. Draw a doodle to represent this experience. Now colour in all these periods and turning points in your life so far, choosing an appropriate colour.

Talk about these turning points in your life with one or two others.

2 Read Luke 19:1–10.
Circle one answer in each section:

A If I had been Zacchaeus when Jesus stopped and asked him to come down, I would have been...

a) flabbergasted
b) scared to death

c) overwhelmed with joy
d) embarrassed
e) excited and afraid

B The most important truth in this story for me is that Jesus...

a) is on the lookout for people 'up a tree'
b) can change a 'climber' into a 'giver'
c) can make a 'little man' big
d) doesn't care what other people think
e) walks into your life and anything can happen

C If Jesus were to pass my way today he would probably...

a) give me a swift kick in the pants
b) put his arm around me and hug me warmly
c) give me a real ding-dong for the way I have been living
d) slap me on the shoulder and tell me I'm OK
e) pass on without saying a thing!

3 As a group, share your answers to each section, and compare the reasons for them.

As a leader, I liked the idea of a DIY group discussion which we could just pick up and get on with. I also liked the informal, light-hearted style. But most of all, I liked the way the study outline gave value to my own story, put it alongside the Bible story and let it be part of the group's learning together.

I discovered that the outline had been produced by an American publisher called Serendipity. The next year I went to visit Lyman Coleman, the founder and writer of these Serendipity Bible studies. This led me in due course to become a partner in Serendipity UK. Working with Scripture Union, we first produced anglicised versions of the American books, then wrote and published our own British material.

There were many variations on the theme, but we always started from the understanding that group Bible study is a different process from studying on your own or listening to a sermon. You are working with others in a group, and groups don't just 'happen' – they need building into small fellowships that people enjoy and want to belong to. Not that these fellowships are an optional extra: they are the basic Christian community where we learn to carry out Jesus' new command, '...love each other as I have loved you' (John 13:34).

The starting point, we understood, was for group members to get to know each other, and the only way to do this was for them to tell each other who they were – in other words, to share their stories. So we built into the early stages of each book or series some simple exercises to help people share their experiences, show the kind of people they were and thus build relationships with the others in the group. But the storytelling didn't stop there. It led on to what we called 'relational' Bible study (we wanted to find another name to replace this bit of jargon, but we failed). It involves seeing how you 'relate' to the Bible passage, by putting yourself into or beside the Bible story and telling the others how you compare or what you would have done in that situation.

This storytelling meets deep personal needs. When we started, we ran into some opposition from reserved English people brought up to think it bad form to talk about yourself. But to 'keep yourself to yourself' leads to emotional starvation. We all need other people to belong to, to share our news with, to try our ideas on, to go out and do things with, to give us a shoulder to cry on, to put us right when we go wrong. Some of us find this support from family, friends or husband/wife. But Christians can also expect to find it in rich measure from our sisters and brothers in God's family.

The beauty of storytelling is that it meets more than one need at once. I need to unburden myself of the struggles I'm having at work or home. And, as I tell my story, I begin to understand who I am and what God may be wanting to make of me. But, at the same time, my story comes as a gift to you because you may be facing a similar problem yourself or trying to help someone who is. As Christians, we grow steadily, with God's help, towards maturity. So the story of our life begins to shift the balance from being mainly a cry for help to becoming more of a cure for other people's ills. Any group will have a mix of 'criers' and 'curers', and the flow of stories between them should release a rich tide of healing.

STORYTELLING IN GROUPS

For many years an acknowledged world expert on how small groups tick has been Dr Roberta Hestenes, Senior Pastor at Solana Beach Presbyterian Church, California. In her course for group leaders, which she developed for Fuller Theological Seminary, she produced a check-list on how to ask the sort of questions that help people share stories from their lives. Here are some key extracts that I have adapted.[2]

Link a request for sharing facts about the self with the emotional response to that fact

For example, start with a question that asks for information or factual material:

> Where did you live when you were twelve?

Then *add* to this a request for personal self-disclosure through *emotional* response:

> Where did you live when you were twelve, and what did you like most about it?

Other examples include:

> When is the first time you remember winning at something important to you, and how did you feel about that?
> What is a good thing happening in your life right now, and what makes it good?
> What is one change you would like to make in your life in the next two years, and why?

Ask questions that call for information which wouldn't be available to other group members...

...unless voluntarily self-disclosed. For example:

> What is a typical Tuesday like for you? Describe your day briefly, beginning with when you get up and when you go to bed. What do you like most and like least in your day?

Characteristics of good questions are:

- They can be understood without explanation. They are clear on their surface, with no vocabulary that has to be defined before people can answer. Simple is best.

- They don't *require* people to confess their sins or share only negative things about themselves. Not – 'What is your worst fault?'

- They can be answered by *every* member of the group. Not – 'When did you graduate from college and what was your degree?'

- They are worth the group taking the time to listen to each other's answers. Not – 'What is your most despised vegetable and why?'

- They help group members to know each other better, and thus to learn to understand and love each other.

- They don't call for a Yes / No response, but for a fuller statement.

- They shouldn't ask for superlatives – the best or the worst – but, rather, one good or one bad experience.

- They allow for enough diversity in response so that each person isn't saying the same thing. Not – 'Who is your favourite preacher and why?' But – 'Who is one person who has influenced you spiritually and how?'

- They ask for personal sharing of the self, *not* for opinions on issues. Not – 'What do you think about abortion?'

Some further tips I would add

Feel free to break a group down into smaller subgroups
Many people are nervous of having more than a handful of people listen to them speak. It is less alarming to tell a story to three

people than to ten: it is often better still to tell it to only one other person. And if you have three small groups working at the same time, you have three times as much talking and sharing going on than if you were all sitting in one circle. You only need to have the whole group together for the times when you are sharing information or doing work that everyone should be part of.

When you subdivide a group, vary who is in each subgroup, so that people get to know everyone else and not just a select few. And keep spouses or flat-sharers apart, as they already know each other's stories.

Have a time of sharing before you plunge into Bible study
Start perhaps with people sharing news. Then get them onto the wavelength of the Bible passage you are going to look at by asking them to share their experience of the topic it is about. For example:

> **Topic:** Prayer
> **Question:** 'When did you first learn about prayer as a child, and what did it mean to you?'
>
> **Topic:** Church membership
> **Question:** 'What were your first impressions of our church, and how did they affect you?'
>
> **Topic:** Creation
> **Question:** 'Where is somewhere you've been for a really good holiday? What was so good about it?'

Use unthreatening questions about daily life rather than a searching inquisition into how good people are as Christians. Memories of childhood are usually interesting and revealing.

Help people think themselves into a Bible story
For example:

> What would you have said and done if you'd been there?
> What would you have done next, after this incident ended?
> What would you have wanted to ask God? What do you want to ask him now?

Then move on to people's own stories and experience
For example:

> When have you been in a similar position?
> What was nice or nasty about it?
> Were you aware of God helping you, and if so, how?
> What light, if any, do you think the Bible story throws
>   on your experience?
> What would you do differently if it happened again?

Remember, this isn't an interrogation of one poor person in front of all the others, but a chance for all to share their stories with a few others.

Think of stories as a present to give people in need
Maybe someone is going into hospital or has just been bereaved. As you pray for each other, someone may be reminded of a memory or an experience that could comfort and reassure. Another person may remember a connected Bible story. Ideally, the atmosphere in your group should be relaxed enough for them to pass these stories on as soon as you finish praying. Group leaders may need to do this themselves once or twice to set a precedent. After that, they could ask from time to time, 'Is there anyone you think you could help or encourage with a story?' It is a good way of expressing our love and care for each other.

Encourage the 'ripple' effect
Once people get used to telling their stories like this, they will start telling them in other settings too. Build up the group's expectations by preparing them to do so. For example:

> Have you ever told that story to the rest of your family?
> Would you be willing to tell the Sunday morning congre-
>   gation what you have just told us?
> What about your friend Sam who's not a Christian –
>   could you tell that story to her?
> Imagine I'm someone you're visiting in hospital – proba-
>   bly dying. I can't read for myself, but I can listen to
>   you. What Bible story would you tell me? Practise
>   telling it now.

In this way, stories of what God did in Bible times and what he is doing now can get around, spreading the good news.

Build up your group story

A group rapidly becomes more than just the sum total of its separate members. It develops a life and a story of its own. As with any human grouping, from the most primitive tribe to the team working on the latest scientific research, the group's story is vital to its continuing life. It enshrines the agreed aims, decisions and values which keep the group together. In the Serendipity studies we began to develop an 'Our Story' section for the group as a whole, alongside the 'My Story' section which focused on the life of each individual. These activities help the group to define why it exists and set ground rules for its shared life. Here, for example, are instructions for a shared group activity in a study of Hannah (1 Sam 1:1–20).[3]

GROUP DESIRES

God granted Hannah her heart's desire and she gave birth to a son. This exercise will help identify what people desire this group to be and what they want it to 'give birth to' or produce. Ask individuals to make two lists on a piece of paper, the first of ways in which this group is like a family, the second of ways in which it is not. Ask them to read their lists to the rest of the group and combine everyone's contributions into two lists on large sheets of paper. Then ask pairs to discuss whether they would like the group to be more or less like a family and specific ways in which they would like it to change. For each change, ask them to try also to identify a realistic way in which that change could be brought about. Discuss these thoughts and desired changes in the whole group and make decisions to implement any changes that everyone in the group would like to see.

Ask individuals to work alone again. Ask them to draw an outline of a baby or give them a prepared outline each. Ask them to draw or write in this outline what they would like to see the group giving 'birth to' – what they would like to see coming out of the group. Stick all the outlines together on one large outline of a baby on a sheet of paper. Talk about the things people have put on the baby.

Finally, give this baby a name. This could be any word at all. It could be a person's name that somehow expresses the aspirations of the group, or some other word or phrase that expresses these aspirations. You could also try and agree on a new name for the group itself that expresses what everyone wants the group to be.

Spot and encourage any especially gifted storytellers

They can have an important part to play in your group or church. Well-told stories – from personal experience, or from the experiences of the whole people of God (in the Bible, or church history, or your own community) – help people to learn, grow, unite and draw on God's resources. The storyteller has been a key leader throughout history in societies where most people can't read, and still is today. Even the New Testament was, for a vital period of twenty or thirty years, in the hands (or mouths) of storytellers. Luke calls them 'the people who saw those things from the beginning and served God by telling people his message' (Luke 1:2). They were the sources for him and others who put the story into writing. But although we have the written Gospels in our 'advanced' world today, many people *don't* read any more than they have to. They more naturally take in information from what they see on television or hear in conversation. The storyteller is in for a comeback.

Take social events like a church party: why not finish them with a story? It could be humorous, or biblical, or something from your own local history, depending on the mood you want to set. Stories are great ways to bond people together at gatherings like this. That's why wedding guests want the bride's father and the best man to reveal highlights of the bride and groom's track records!

• Things to do

Here are some activities for a group to do together, to encourage confidence and skill in telling stories.

TALK ABOUT YOURSELF AND YOUR EXPERIENCES

Group people in pairs, so that they talk to just one other person. Ask them to speak for only sixty seconds before you interrupt and give them a rest. Later, you can build this up to two minutes, three, even five. At first, give them very simple, factual topics to talk about, for example:

> What I had for breakfast this morning.
> What happened on my way to this meeting.
> Why I chose the shoes I'm wearing.

As they get used to it, move on to longer topics, for example:

> My day or week so far.
> A television programme I've enjoyed recently.
> A holiday or day out I remember clearly.
> A person who's had a big influence on me.

With practice and growing confidence, you can build up the audience to three or four. And you can extend the topic to a slice of your life-story, for example:

> Something that not many people know about me.
> Something that happened to me as a child which has had
>   a big effect on me.
> How Christian faith became real for me.
> A problem I'm facing at the moment.

PRACTISE TELLING STORIES

Tell each other jokes. They are often in story form, and are well-shaped so as to get a laugh.

GET PEOPLE USED TO TELLING BIBLE STORIES OUT LOUD

In his book, *Story Journey*, Thomas Boomershine gives this advice:[4]

> The best way to get people involved in telling stories is to lead a group through the stages of learning and telling a story ... Learning a story with a group is great fun. And the best introduction to learning a biblical story is for

people to get physically and emotionally involved as a group in some kind of fun. The essential component is give and take, action and response. A 'lion hunt' has become my most frequent starting point ... the group says and does everything that the leader says and does, in immediate response ... The gestures are big and boisterous and can only be learned by doing them. Most camp leaders and kindergarten teachers can initiate you into this august oral tradition ... after the applause and laughter dies down, go through exactly the same process with [a Bible] story. The biblical story needs the same energy in its words and gestures. Keep the word groups fairly short. The group says the story back to you with the gestures...

Hand out the story [written] in episodes and explain that after the next round of repetition, each person will tell the story to a partner. This is a typical introduction:

After ... we go through it together again, I'm going to ask you to turn immediately and tell it to your partner ... If you get lost, your partner will help you. Partners, don't look at the paper ... The paper is only an aid to your memory ... Therefore, while your partners are telling the story, remember along with them. Listen. If they get lost, just pick them up at that point. If neither one of you can remember, then you look and refresh your partner's memory.

Take these fifteen minutes to tell the story back and forth as often as you can. Work toward getting through it with as high a degree of mastery and comfort as possible. Don't talk about it. We have spent years learning how to talk about these stories and almost no time learning how to tell them. Concentrate on the story ... Our aim is for everyone to be able to get through the story from beginning to end.

After fifteen minutes ... call the group back. A brief period of feedback is always helpful. The main task is to celebrate the group's achievement.

USE BIBLE STORIES TO HELP MEET PASTORAL NEEDS

Give each person in the group a card with a pastoral need on it, for example 'Moving to live somewhere else', 'Sick child', 'Divorce'. The rest of the group then think of possible Bible stories to tell that person, to remind them of God's comfort and strength. Choose one of the stories and have one person in the group tell the story as a gift to the person in need. You may find it helpful to read the story from the Bible first.

Think about people you know who really are in pastoral need. Discuss how you could remind them of a helpful Bible story. Do you know them well enough to tell them face to face or to ring up? Could you write them a note? Or lend them a tape of the story being read? Don't leave the discussion without praying for God to find a way to meet their needs.

COMPARE PRESENT EXPERIENCE WITH BIBLE STORIES

In small groups, each person in turn tells the others about a recent experience. It should be something important to them – a success, a problem, a celebration, a concern. Each of the others should then refer to a Bible story they have been reminded of or which in some way connects with the person's experience. 'Left-brain' people will find it natural to think of reasons why the two stories connect, but 'right-brain' people should be encouraged to follow their own intuition. The group together explores what parallels there are between the Bible story and the modern experience, and whether there is anything to learn from this.

SEE YOUR OWN LIFE AS PART OF GOD'S STORY

In his book, *The Adventure Begins*, Terry Clutterham writes:[5]

> Think about your own life in the context of the whole history of creation and the vast plan God has for it. What important part are you playing in it all? Try telling the story of the whole Bible story in brief, making sure that you include your own life in the part that comes before Jesus' return.
>
> You may find you want to pray about what you have been thinking.

• Quotes

Human beings are storytellers, and without stories we
would not be human ... We know we are more than
mere hairless bipeds because of our parables, jokes,
sagas, fairy tales, myths, fables, epics and yarns. Religion
should be the seedbed and spawning ground of stories.
But today religion is not fulfilling its storytelling role.

Harvey Cox, The Seduction of the Spirit,
Wildwood House, 1974, pp11–12

During times of crisis, and this is one, we desperately
need reflection and clarity of vision. To act with presence
of mind. Let us therefore encourage one another to
keep still long enough and In sufficiently lovely ways.
Return to our own still centre. To be inspired. To rekin-
dle our love.

Whenever stories are told, stillness falls. We cease
our restless frittering. During these times of concentrated devotion to alternative realms we may reconnect
with the power of creation. We rest momentarily.
Through such resting we are renewed. Renewal inspires
the courage to change.

Alida Gersie, Earthtales, Green Print, 1991

After a day spent in the emergency room of a city hospital, a day in which I was surrounded by accidents, dying
children, irritable patients, many of whom spoke no
English and could not follow directions, incredible
patience on the part of understaffed doctors and nurses,
I felt somewhat the same sense of irrationality in the
world around me (all these people were there by acci-
dent) as did the man who was almost killed by the falling
beam. Whenever this occurs I turn to the piano, to my
typewriter, to a book. We turn to stories and pictures
and music because they show us who and what and why
we are, and what our relationship is to life and death,
what is essential, and what, despite the arbitrariness of
falling beams, will not burn. Paul Klee said, 'Art does not
reproduce the visible. Rather, it makes visible.' It is not

then, at its best, a mirror but an icon. It takes the chaos in which we live and shows us structure and pattern, not the structure of conformity which imprisons but the structure which liberates, sets us free to become growing, mature human beings.

Madeleine L'Engle, A Circle of Quiet,
The Crosswicks Journal Book 1,
Harper and Row, 1972, pp120–121

Telling a story to another person or group, face to face, is different from reading a book. It has its own unique dynamics. Storytelling is fun, engaging, spontaneous, and playful. To say, 'Let me tell you a story' is like saying 'Let's go play' ... Storytelling creates community. Persons who tell each other stories become friends ... Storytelling is also highly emotional. To laugh and to cry, to be deeply moved and to get so involved that you have to know how the story came out in the end – that is storytelling ... And the stories you remember and tell to others become the best gifts you have to give. They become yours in a special way. People become the stories they love to tell.

Thomas Boomershine, Story Journey, pp18–19

• Resources

TELL ME A STORY
During 1997 Footprints Theatre Trust are setting up a new initiative called Storymine. This is a community story-sharing project aiming to 'give people the opportunity, through story-making, to enrich and enliven their community life, and value its spiritual and moral character'. The idea is:

• To enable community members to discover and tell their own 'story', whether fact or fiction.
• To aid understanding of oneself and of others.
• To have fun!

The plan is to pilot the concept in one area, then make the experience available for other areas to do something similar.

For information, contact **Steve Stickley, Footprints Theatre Trust, 79 Maid Marian Way, Nottingham NG1 6AE, tel 0115 958 6554**. Steve introduces the concept like this:

We may not think our own story very interesting, let alone compelling. Perhaps this is because we feel it is so familiar already or that maybe others would not be interested because it is too ordinary.

Every human life is unique. Every moment of every day is different to the next. Every set of circumstances is never to be repeated. Only change is constant. All over our planet in the course of one lifetime there are billions of people in millions of situations with thousands of relationships, an infinite variety. Given these permutations the idea of any one person being 'ordinary' starts to seem ridiculous. We all see life differently and we all have something to say or questions to ask. And when we do, our imaginations are already at work.

Someone asks you, 'How was your holiday?' and, before you know what's happened, you have launched into a description of the weather, the place you stayed, what the food was like and the day you locked the keys inside the car. As you bring these details to mind you relive them to a certain extent but, more importantly, you decide *how* to construct the story depending upon whom you are telling. The same details are told differently to your next door neighbour as they are to your boss. We are, all of us, quite expert storytellers in our own way.

'Surely stories aren't that important?'

Can you imagine what would happen if they didn't exist? How would you go about describing your holiday then? Would our conversation be made up of nothing but information? How would children learn to read? How could we describe our feelings, wishes and ambitions if we couldn't compare them to anything?

To take away story is to take away our imaginations altogether. Language might as well not exist. We would become just another species of ape screeching and gesturing to one another.

Stories encapsulate the entire scope of human experience. Through sharing and listening to stories we engage in rehearsing and reliving all human activity. The story is our way of understanding and expressing emotions, dreams, identity, morality, philosophy and spirituality.

Story makes us human beings.

WRITE YOUR OWN LIFE STORY

A Christian, Mike Oke, helps people write their own life stories to give as a present to friends and family. He has a series of questions to help jog their memories. He helps them write them up in an interesting way. He then produces them in a presentation book illustrated with photographs.

'I do think memories are worth writing down,' he says. 'All the family recollections disappear unless you do so.'

For further information, contact **Bound Biographies, 23 Thompson Drive, Bicester OX6 9FA, tel 01869 321727**.

• Notes

1   Reprinted by kind permission from Group Bible study books by Lyman Coleman, published by Serendipity House.

2   Adapted from *Building Christian Community Through Small Groups*, by Dr Roberta Hestenes, Fuller Theological Seminary (US). © Roberta Hestenes 1985.

3   Chris Powell with Anton Baumohl, Joan King and Lance Pierson, *Families of God*, Small Group Resources and Scripture Union, 1994, p44.

4   Thomas Boomershine, *Story Journey*, Abingdon Press, 1988, pp53–59.

5   Terry Clutterham, *The Adventure Begins*, Scripture Union / CPAS, 1996, p140.

5 Stories in the Bible

It was my first term in the juniors. At the end of term we had a carol service, and the tradition was that one of the new children each year did a reading. They tried three of us and chose me. My reading was the story of the shepherds hearing about Jesus and going to see him (Luke 2:8–20). We had to read from a lectern, but I was so tiny I had to climb on a box to see the Bible. I felt nervous, but it went well. When I finished, I knew this was something I could do. Not like playing the piano in public: when I tried *that*, my hands shook so much they played the wrong notes!

In my own mind I became quite an expert Bible reader. Going on to senior school, I didn't think much of the teachers and prefects who usually read in our assemblies. I enjoyed doing impressions of their stumblings and wrong pronunciations. But one day in my last year I met my match.

We took our school play on a tour around Holland, and on the Sunday we went to the English-speaking church. The chaplain was an old man with a rich, deep voice, and he did the Bible reading himself. It was the story of Naaman (2 Kings 5) – wonderfully dramatic, and he made the most of it. The king of Syria sends his great general to the king of Israel to be healed. I can still see and hear (in the words of the Authorised or King James version that we all used then) the king's terrified reaction as the chaplain read it:

> Am I God, to kill and to make alive, that this man doth send unto me to recover a man of his leprosy? wherefore consider, I pray you, and see how he seeketh a quarrel against me.

He was just as good at expressing Naaman's mortified pride:

> Behold, I thought, He will surely come out to me, and
> stand, and call on the name of the Lord his God, and
> strike his hand over the place, and recover the leper…

But Elisha does no such thing: he just sends word that Naaman
should take a dip in the Jordan!

> Are not Abana and Pharpar, rivers of Damascus, better
> than all the waters of Israel? may I not wash in them,
> and be clean?

The chaplain's voice was now trembling with indignation.
And, finally, the devastating ending. Elisha's servant, his eye
on the main chance, collars Naaman's payment for himself:

> But he went in, and stood before his master. And Elisha
> said unto him, Whence comest thou, Gehazi? And he
> said, Thy servant went no whither. And he said unto
> him, Went not mine heart with thee, when the man
> turned again from his chariot to meet thee? Is it a time
> to receive money, and to receive garments, and olive-
> yards, and vineyards, and sheep, and oxen, and menser-
> vants, and maidservants? The leprosy therefore of
> Naaman shall cleave unto thee, and unto thy seed for
> ever.

Long pause, hushed voice.

> And he went out from his presence a leper as white as
> snow.

An even longer pause before he said, 'Here endeth the lesson.'
You could hear our gasp of relief after holding our breath for that
appalled silence. Budding actors ourselves, we knew we had been
watching a master of the art, more experienced than any of us. But
what impressed me most was that he took the story utterly seriously. It told of a God you can't cheat or trifle with. And, through
the reader's words, this God was right there in the atmosphere all
around us. I felt uncomfortable, awed, even a little frightened. But
even more I felt, 'I want to be able to read the Bible like that.'

I couldn't have put this into words then, but what had happened was that God had spoken to us through the reading of his story. Surely this shouldn't be a rare event, happening once in a blue moon. If we believe the Bible is in a unique sense the word of God, we should *expect* him to speak through it. Every time. This is what this chapter is about – trying to ensure that when we read the Bible in our services, God speaks.

• SPEAKING GOD'S WORDS

Most of what follows will apply to any passage from the Bible, but as this is a book about storytelling I will focus on the special challenge of Bible narratives – the parts that tell a story and include conversations. The changes of voice, mood and scene make these narratives harder to read than the rest of the Bible. Old Testament prophecy and New Testament letters are simply messages from a speaker to a group of God's people, so they are easier than narratives to pick up and read straight.

So what can we do to 'bring back God's word' into our Bible readings? It is a question of asking the right questions in the right order. Many churches start with the question 'How?', but we need to go back further than that and beging with 'Why?' and 'Who?'

• Why?

This is the number one question that should be asked about all our church activities. Everything else follows on from the answer. Why do we read the Bible in church services? Because these are the special stories and writings God has given us to learn from. They tell us who he is and what he is like. He used the Old Testament scriptures and the New Testament gospel to give birth to the church, and he wants to go on using them now so that we can have life and strength as we serve him. God continues to speak to us through them.

Surely this must be at the very heart of why we meet. All our praises and prayers, our efforts to serve each other in love, flow from this basic fact that God is with us and speaking to us. Our efforts are secondary: *he* is primary.

Even, dare I say it, preaching is secondary. Any teaching we do should be based on the Bible: it will be authoritative only if it is faithful to scripture. So the Bible reading should come first not just in the order of events but in our order of priorities.[1] If our aim, prayers and planning for the service begin with the Bible reading, then everything else will flow from it, including the sermon or story or whatever form the preaching / teaching takes. This is a controversial idea, but even where people agree with it in theory they seldom reflect it in practice. Bible reading has become in most churches a mere appendage of the sermon. It is usually a short foretaste, unremarkable and unremarked. There would be little difference if it didn't happen at all. The real Bible work happens in the preaching: that's where the passage is explored, analysed, taught, handled with reverence and love. But the Bible has its own preaching power, and it should be let loose to do its work whenever it is read. The Jews of Jesus' day seem to me to have had the right balance.

> Jesus travelled to Nazareth, where he had grown up. On the Sabbath day he went to the synagogue, as he always did, and stood up to read.

This was the custom – standing to show reverence for God's word.

> The book of Isaiah the prophet was given to him. He opened the book and found the place where this is written:
> 'The Lord has put his Spirit in me,
> because he appointed me to tell the Good News to the poor.
> He has sent me to tell the captives they are free
> and to tell the blind that they can see again.
> God sent me to free those who have been treated unfairly
> and to announce the time when the Lord will show his kindness.'
> Jesus closed the book, gave it back to the assistant and sat down. Everyone in the synagogue was watching Jesus closely.

Another spellbound silence. But Jesus wasn't sitting back down in the congregation. He was sitting down to preach!

He began to say to them, 'While you heard these words
just now, they were coming true.'

Luke 4:16–21

Stand up to read the Bible, sit down to talk about it – that was the
usual practice (Matt 5:1; 13:1–2; 26:55; Mark 9:35; Acts 16:13).[2]
And when he does talk about it, Jesus says that something happened when he read the words of the Bible: God made them come
true. Shouldn't we expect God always to do something with his
words when we read them?

This way of reading is vitally important. It is not an outdated
irrelevance in an age when most people can read on their own.
Reading aloud takes us back to the original sound and feel of the
New Testament. The epistles were read aloud to the churches they
addressed. The Gospels record the stories of Jesus that the apostles were proclaiming in their preaching. And, at that time, the Old
Testament was always heard aloud too. Students at Jewish schools
were forbidden to read their sacred books silently. They reckoned
the scriptures only came alive and had proper effect if read out
loud.

So the human voice is the original, authentic instrument for
communicating the Bible. It is also, still, the market leader. More
people hear the Bible being read to them than ever read it for
themselves: children in school assemblies; people in our services
on the fringe of church life; visitors to baptisms, weddings or
funerals; the huge audience for services on radio and television,
including national institutions like carols from King's College,
Cambridge. What an opportunity for good or ill. How important
to read with life and power.

But show me the church today who treats the Bible reading as
the high spot of their services. Show me the Bible reader who
works as hard at preparing the reading as the preacher does at the
sermon.

• Who?

If the Bible reading is such a sacred moment, who should do it?

Here again, many churches have allowed traditions to go
unquestioned for a long time. In some, the automatic choice to
read is the preacher, who then expounds the passage. There is a

lot to be said for this. Preachers study the passage closely when preparing the sermon. They spend time with it until it begins to grip them. They form an idea of what God wants them to say about it. So they know how to introduce the reading. They know which words or sections to emphasise. They naturally tie the reading and the sermon in together. It seems a sensible economy of effort. But it means that one person is responsible for a large chunk of the service. In churches who have only one regular preacher – or a stream of visiting preachers – it denies the Bible reading to other church members.

Other churches leave the Bible reading in the hands of a few senior and prominent leaders – assistant ministers, elders, deacons, wardens, council members, whatever name they use. These are the people to look up to, so it is fitting they should set the tone. But other churches adopt exactly the opposite policy. They see the Bible reading as the part of the service 'almost anyone' can do. It takes special skill and training to preach, to lead the music, or even to lead the prayers. But reading the Bible is the birthright of the ordinary church member. It is a mark of the New Testament age that 'all kinds of people' will speak God's word (Acts 2:17). And it is a good way of introducing people to leading up front – the less pushy church members, newcomers, new Christians and children.

All these approaches are useful, some better for some occasions than others. At a popular community carol service, for instance, it may be good to have as readers people who are well-known in the community. However, your system will become bad if it gets rigid and stifles the freedom to choose the most suitable readers for each meeting and for each passage.

As it is harder to read narrative passages than others, I suggest we give them special treatment. There are several alternatives on offer.

ONE VOICE

If we stick with a single reader, let's make sure it is a gifted reader. According to Paul, the spiritual gift of his assistant Timothy was a God-given ability 'to read the Scriptures to the people, strengthen them, and teach them' (1 Tim 4:13–14). He was an early example of the reader and preacher combined. But in my experience there are people today who are gifted readers but not preachers (or, at least, not yet). You probably know who they are in your church. They make you listen. Their gift is partly natural – they make sense of the words, their voices carry, and they make the story live. But the gift is also spiritual – when they read, you know that God is here, speaking to you. Of course, loving God and wanting to read are more important than having a purely natural skill. But with Bible stories I would want a reader with both natural ability and spiritual zeal, not just one or the other.

I know of one church with a specially gifted reader who they get to do the reading nearly every week. It may or may not be right to use your gifted readers all the time, but I wonder if they know that your church leaders recognise and value their gift, and are thinking about the best times to use it. I think these gifted readers should be strong contenders for reading story passages.

TWO OR MORE VOICES

A gifted reader can do amazing things to lift any Bible passage off the page and bring it to life in front of people – in other words, to be God's mouthpiece. But they shouldn't normally be left to read story passages on their own. And *un*gifted readers certainly shouldn't! I know it's the custom in the vast majority of churches to have just one reader per reading, but with a story passage it is quite simply a bad custom. There are better ways to do it.

Dramatised

Some people take fright at the word 'drama', as if we were trying to play around with God's book or improve on it. But all I mean here is setting the story out like a play script, starting each speech on a new line. Very few Bible stories are nothing but the words of the storyteller. Almost always at least one of the characters in the story says something. In real life this meant that there was a different voice from the storyteller's. So it is a step more realistic, a step closer to how the story first took place, to share the reading between two voices. More lifelike still, of course, is to use a separate reader for each person who speaks.

There is a helpful book, *The Dramatised Bible*, which sets out all the main Bible passages for this kind of reading. It would be a good investment for every church to have a copy. This is how it presents the middle part of the Naaman story:[3]

Narrator	Naaman, when he was cured, returned to Elisha with all his men and said:
Naaman	Now I know that there is no god but the God of Israel; so please, sir, accept a gift from me.
Narrator	Elisha answered:
Elisha	By the living Lord, whom I serve, I swear that I will not accept a gift.
Narrator	Naaman insisted that he accept it, but he would not. So Naaman said:
Naaman	If you won't accept my gift, then let me have two mule-loads of earth to take home with me, because from now on I will not offer sacrifices or burnt-offerings to any god except the Lord. So I hope that the Lord will forgive me when I accompany my king to the temple of Rimmon, the god of Syria, and worship him. Surely the Lord will forgive me!
Elisha	Go in peace.
Narrator	Naaman left. He had gone only a short distance, when Elisha's servant Gehazi said to himself:
Gehazi	My master has let Naaman get away without paying a thing! He should have accepted what that Syrian offered him. By the living Lord, I will run after him and get something from him.

So, four voices instead of one. Once you understand the technique, you can do it for any story passage. Obviously, it takes a bit longer to practise because you need to get the readers together. But how can we expect to do a job well without taking the time to practise?

If the extra readers are confident and experienced actors, it is natural to add another level of reality, to start moving and acting the story out. The Elisha story contains conversations, gestures, actions and at least ten different scenes. If it is really difficult to hear in your church building and you have only got stand-microphones, readers may need to stay still while others mime the action. More work again, but how rewarding to let people see the story as well as hear it.

Choral and congregational

The next challenge comes when the story includes a chorus, that is, words spoken together by a group or crowd. The Christmas story I read all on my own as a junior appears like this in *The Dramatised Bible*:[4]

Narrator	Suddenly a great company of the heavenly host appeared with the angel, praising God.
Chorus (joyfully)	Glory to God in the highest and on earth peace to all on whom his favour rests.
Narrator	When the angels had left them and gone into heaven, the shepherds said to one another:
Shepherd I	Let's go to Bethlehem –
Shepherd 2	And see this thing that has happened –
Shepherd 3	Which the Lord has told us about.

This contains two choruses – the angels and the shepherds – and the editor has tried a different approach with each. He has divided the shepherds' words among three readers: we don't know how many shepherds there were, but three works quite well as an all-purpose number to suggest a group. The angels, on the other hand, he leaves to speak together in unison. This will mean more time in practice, but for how many people? You can't really get away with three here, because Luke calls them 'a great company of the heavenly host'! At a special Christmas service, it may be worth going for broke – use all the children to say these words, or the members of your choir / singing group.

But if that sounds over the top, at least in an ordinary service, why not do what we do in my church? We use the congregation for crowd scenes or choral reading. We have Bibles in the seats, which we ask people to open. Then we simply say, 'Follow carefully and join in at verse 14 – you're the angels!'

Or, if we want to be more ambitious, we give them a choral reading like the one below, printed out on a sheet. We practised this the week before with the children, who then helped lead from the front. But for everyone else it was instant reading on the spot. This is bringing the Bible reading from the front into the middle

of the congregation. It helps them do more than hear and see; they
are now part of it. Words from the Bible are in **bold**, the others
are responses to them.[5]

HE ASCENDED INTO HEAVEN

Narrator	Jesus **led them out of the city as far as Bethany, where he raised his hands and blessed them.**
Children	*(kneel, and then)* He blessed us.
Narrator	**As he was blessing them, he departed from them and was taken up into heaven.**
Children	*(look up, stand up, point and then)* GASP!
Narrator	**They still had their eyes fixed on the sky as he went away, when two men dressed in white suddenly stood beside them.**
All	GASP!!
Angels	**Galileans, why are you standing there looking up at the sky?**
Children	Why at the sky?
Angels	**This Jesus, who was taken from you into heaven will come back in the same way that you saw him go to heaven.**
Children	He went into heaven.
Adults	He will come back.
Narrator	**They worshipped him –**
Adults	Bow low and submit to him. *(Children bow.)*
Narrator	**and went back into Jerusalem –**
Children	Run, skip and jump there. *(Children run to centre of congregation.)*
Narrator	**Filled with great joy –**
Children	HIP HIP HALLELUJAH!
Narrator	**And spent all their time in the Temple giving –**
Children	**Thanks to God.**
Adults	*(louder)* Thanks to God!

Adults 2	*(louder)* Thanks to God!
Narrator	This is the word of the Lord —
All	*(loudest)* THANKS TO GOD!

This is treating the words rather as a composer treats music. The simplest form is to give 'chorus' words to various sections of the congregation. But as you grow more adventurous, you may come to feel that some of the words are so important, they are worth repeating. You can then use different sections of the 'choir' to echo key words and phrases. You can play with loud and soft, light and shade to fit the mood of the words. Build up to full volume by joining all the sections together, one after another. Finally, with experience, you may feel it is appropriate sometimes to add words and actions to highlight biblical words and give them another dimension.

A simpler way to create some of the same effects, especially good for all-age services, is the 'response story'. Here one or two people tell the story but the congregation respond to key words with prearranged sounds or actions. This can become quite funny and anarchic, so it works best with happy stories that no one will mind treating light-heartedly.[6] Teach the congregation their responses before you begin, and leave a list of them on a flipchart or overhead projector. Perhaps you could also have a rehearsed group up in front leading them. Here is an example from *Acting Up* by Dave Hopwood:[7]

GIDEON

Responses

Gideon	Who me?
Winepress	Squelch, squelch
Angel	Flap, flap (wings)
Frightened	Bite nails
Midianites	Boo
Smallest	Aah

There was once a young man called GIDEON.
    Yes. And GIDEON, oh yes, worked in a WINEPRESS.
And GIDEON, that's the one, didn't have a lot of courage, in fact, most of the time he was very FRIGHTENED, because he was the SMALLEST person in his family. But

one day, while he was in the WINEPRESS, he saw an ANGEL, who said to him:

'Hello, GIDEON.'

'Yes, you,' said the ANGEL, 'I've got a job for you.'

'But I've already got one – in this WINEPRESS,' said GIDEON. And he was now very FRIGHTENED. After all, he was the SMALLEST person in his whole family.

The ANGEL replied, 'Now listen, GIDEON. Yes, you. I want you to go and fight the MIDIANITIES.'

'The ... the ... the ... MIDIANITES?' said GIDEON. 'Yes – you!'

'But the reason I'm in this WINEPRESS, is so that I can get away from the MIDIANITES. I mean, the MIDI-ANITES, are big ... and bad! And I'm only the SMALL-EST person in my family and, most important, I'm FRIGHTENED.'

'No need to be,' said the ANGEL, 'God will help you, GIDEON. Yes. You.' ...

As this example shows, it usually helps to retell the Bible story in your own words. That way you make sure the key words keep coming fast and furious. Aim to have them often enough for people to pick them up and enjoy them, but not so often that they get boring. For devising your own responses, note that some choose themselves (*Boo* and *Aah*), some are sound effects (*Squelch* and *Flap*) and some try to express the heart of the story or of a character (*Who me?*).

• How?

Whoever does the reading and however many, there are minimum standards we must demand from those standing up front. It is embarrassing if they stumble over words and names and obviously don't know what they mean. If they read in a flat, uninterested voice, they will switch the rest of us off from hearing God's voice. This would make a nonsense of what should be the peak of the whole service. Asking people to read the Bible to others is giving them a high and holy task. We are asking them to speak God's words to us. We need to help them prepare worthily, not just skim through it.

READING THE BIBLE IN CHURCH

Beginners, start here

Your church probably gives instructions on how to do the readings in your services. But here are my quick suggestions which you might like to compare with them.[8]

PREPARING IN ADVANCE

Pray for God's help

As you read you will be voicing God's word to his people and passing on a message that can change their lives. You will be bringing them good news of hope, comfort and challenge. Ask God to give you enthusiasm for this exciting chance to serve him and them.

Read the passage several times so you get to know it

As a reader, you have three great aims:

- To make the meaning clear to the listeners. Ask for help if you don't understand something in the text. Check and practise any words or names that are difficult to pronounce.

- To convey something of what the story has come to mean to you. Ask what message God is bringing to you through it. Then let that message colour your attitude as you read: 'I've had a preview of this story, and now I want to share it with you'. This will naturally seep through into your tone of voice.

- To lift the story off the page and give it to the congregation. Look up at them as much as you can. You need to know the story well enough to take a phrase in at a glance and then say it without reading it word for word. If it helps, follow the passage with your finger, so your eyes go back to the right place each time you look down.

Be ready to introduce the story

Set the scene or explain who it's about. It may be good to work with the preacher on this. Work out what you want to say, and write it down.

At the beginning of the story, change 'he' or 'she' to the name of the character...

...if it isn't clear.

Practise aloud!

This is essential, to get over the shock of hearing your own voice and to make any natural mistakes where it doesn't matter.

Until you are experienced, practise in your church building. If you have a microphone, get it switched on. Learn where you need to stand and how loud to speak for it to pick you up. Ask someone to sit at the back and stop you if they can't hear – obviously it is a waste of everyone's time if you can't be heard. The commonest faults are to read too fast and to drop your voice at the end of sentences. Speak more slowly than you expect, and put effort into it right up to the final full stop.

GETTING READY BEFORE THE SERVICE STARTS

To read well, you need to be as confident and unflustered as possible. Meet the other leaders of the service to pray with them: this helps you to focus on God and put things in his hands right from the start. Check that you know when the reading comes in the service. Mark the place in the Bible you will be using. And keep yourself a seat within easy reach of where you are going to be reading, for example at the end of a row.

THE READING ITSELF

Remember – this is God's story from God's book. Do everything to fit in with such an exciting and purposeful moment.

Get into position in good time

For example, during the last verse of the song before. Make yourself comfortable and secure with feet slightly apart. Put your weight on your toes, not your heels: this opens your diaphragm for better breathing. Take a couple of deep breaths to steady any nerves and give yourself plenty of puff. Look at the people you will be reading to and establish a rapport with them.

Allow people to settle before you start
Relax and remind yourself not to hurry.

Announce the reading
Do this in whatever is your church's usual way. If people have
Bibles to look it up in, wait until they have found the place. Then
give any introduction you have prepared.

Read the passage
Remember what you have practised: slow, clear and alive. Taking
plenty of time over the reading helps all round: it shows the
importance of the Bible's words, helps you to relax and the congregation to follow and grasp the meaning.

Pause to let the words sink in
Then finish in the usual way ('This is the word of the Lord...').
Wait for any response from the congregation, then return to your
seat without hurrying.

Growing more experienced

Even if you have a gift for reading the Bible, you won't be an
expert the first time you do it – or the twenty-first. It was one of
Timothy's spiritual gifts, but Paul told him, 'Continue to do those
things; give your life to doing them so your progress may be seen
by everyone' (1 Tim 4:15). We all need to learn and make
progress.

There is science and skill in reading aloud. It isn't enough just
to 'read the words'. Their meaning comes over not by simply saying them, but by –

- Putting expression into them
- Grouping them in phrases
- Stressing some words more than others

Each of these helps us make the meaning of the words clearer. And
our aim should be to be so clear that no one can misunderstand
what is being read. So we need to work at expression, phrasing and
stress. Don't just leave it to inspiration or your memory at the time:
this is not the way to give of your best. Practise and mark your
copy of the words with reminders and instructions that you can

read. You may have a Bible you don't mind writing in, or it might be better to make an enlarged photocopy on paper thick enough to mark with highlighters. Best of all, especially with stories we think we know well, is to write or type them out ourselves. This forces us to look at the words and think how we will say them.

EXPRESSION

Expression takes black-on-white words and turns them into colour. It takes cold print and makes it warm. It takes the two-dimensional page and gives it height and depth. The precision tools of expression are what we looked at in chapter one – volume, pace, pitch and tone or mood. Let's look at an example of each in the Christmas story in Luke 2. (For these I am again using *The Dramatised Bible* which takes the NIV text for the Christmas story.)

Volume
The story is full of praising:

> Suddenly a great company of the heavenly host appeared with the angel, praising God…
> The shepherds returned, glorifying and praising God for all the things they had heard and seen…

I suppose you can praise God quietly, but these verses should definitely be read loudly.

Pace
Follow the natural accelerations and decelerations in the story:

> [FAST] So they hurried off and [SLOW] found Mary and Joseph, and the baby, who was lying in the manger.
> [FAST] When they had seen him, they spread the word concerning what had been told them about this child, and all who heard it were amazed at what the shepherds said to them. [SLOW] But Mary treasured up all these things and pondered them in her heart.

Pitch
Use your voice to paint the height / depth dimension – up to heaven and down to earth:

[UP] Glory to God in the highest
[DOWN] and on earth peace to all on whom his favour
rests.

Tone / Mood

Look for the words which tell us the emotions people felt:

An angel of the Lord appeared to them, and the glory of
the Lord shone around them, and they were *terrified*...
When they had seen him, they spread the word concerning what had been told them about this child, and all
who heard it were *amazed*...

Think yourself back into those feelings. Get inside the terror and
amazement they felt. Then let it spill out in your tone of voice.
The Dramatised Bible is designed to help people to read in public, so sometimes it adds an instruction about the tone:

Chorus   Glory to God in the highest
(joyfully)   and on earth peace to all on whom his favour
                   rests.

Don't feel limited to those occasional hints. Look for the right
tone for every speech. What mood do you think is right, for
instance, for the first angel's speech?

Do not be afraid. I bring you good news of great joy that
will be for all the people. Today in the town of David a
Saviour has been born to you; he is Christ the Lord. This
will be a sign to you: You will find a baby wrapped in
cloths and lying in a manger.

PHRASING AND PAUSING

Long sentences need breaking down into smaller units or you will
run out of breath. Try reading this sentence without a break:

When they had seen him, they spread the word concerning what had been told them about this child, and all
who heard it were amazed at what the shepherds said
to them.

You not only put a strain on your lungs, you make it harder for your hearers to understand because you are cramming too much of the story into one speech unit. People can only take in at one mental gulp about the same number of words as we can comfortably speak in one breath. Each group of words that forms one of these units for speaking and understanding is called a *phrase*.[9] The long sentence above contains three phrases, each reporting a further stage of the story:

[1] When they had seen him, [2] they spread the word concerning what had been told them about this child, and [3] all who heard it were amazed at what the shepherds said to them.

In reading aloud, you mark each phrase by taking a moment's *pause* at the end. If you also need to take a breath, that's the time for it.

A correctly placed pause makes the meaning clear and helps the listeners to grasp it. But pause in the wrong place, or fail to pause in the right place, and you will blur or even change the meaning. The old King James version of this story – the version I had to read at my school carol service when I was eight – contains the most famous graveyard for unwary readers.

And they came with haste, and found Mary, and Joseph, and the babe lying in a manger.

Unless you paused carefully, you pushed Mary and Joseph into the manger with Jesus! All modern translators, thankfully, are aware of this and do their best to help you with the phrasing. But it's still worth watching your step.

So they hurried off and found Mary and Joseph, and the baby, *who was* lying in the manger.

So how do we know where phrases begin and end? There are two ways: picking up the clues when the writers guide us, and making our own judgment when they don't!

The writer's clue: punctuation

Punctuation marks are the writer's guide to phrasing. Semi-colons, colons and full stops call for a definite pause. A new paragraph means a change of speaker, or even a change of time and place, and so needs a slightly longer pause and a breath. If you want to mark your copy, good signs are | for an ordinary pause, || for a double.

Angel	Do not be afraid.	I bring you good news of great joy that will be for all the people.	Today in the town of David a Saviour has been born to you;	he is Christ the Lord.	This will be a sign to you:	You will find a baby wrapped in cloths and lying in a manger. ||
Narrator	Suddenly a great company of the heavenly host appeared with the angel, praising God.

The editor of *The Dramatised Bible* has added the instruction 'PAUSE' at one point where he feels we need more than an ordinary full stop.

...all who heard it were amazed at what the shepherds said to them. (PAUSE) But Mary treasured up all these things and pondered them in her heart.

It is a contrast and change of mood worthy of a ||, even if not quite a new paragraph.

Commas are much less reliable, because no two writers use them in quite the same way. It is usually safe to say that a comma in the Bible means the end of a phrase, and you should give a half-pause. A way to mark it is like this ´.

Suddenly a great company of the heavenly host appeared with the angel, ´ praising God. |

But there is no rule that says you must pause at commas, and there is one common case where you must not.

This is the difference between a defining phrase and a describing phrase. They usually begin with 'who', 'which' or 'that' and sometimes have a comma before them. Our Luke 2 passage contains one of each of the 'who' variety.

> Glory to God in the highest
> and on earth peace to all *on whom his favour rests*...
>> So they hurried off and found Mary and Joseph, and
> the baby, *who was lying in the manger.*

A *describing* phrase simply adds extra information about the person or thing being described. The sentence would still mean essentially the same without it. 'So they hurried off and found Mary and Joseph, and the baby. Oh, by the way, you might also like to know, the baby was lying in the manger.' This is a separate piece of information and you should pause before it. *Always pause before a describing phrase.*

> So they hurried off and found Mary and Joseph, | and the
> baby, ´ who was lying in the manger.

But a *defining* phrase tells us something vital we can't do without. If we leave it out, we change the meaning or make nonsense. 'Glory to God in the highest and on earth peace to *all*' is not what the angels said or meant. They didn't mean *all without exception.* They said, '...all *on whom his favour rests*'. The 'on whom' phrase *defines* the 'all' and we can't do without it. If you pause before it, you will cause confusion. Give it to us without the hint of a pause.

> ...on earth peace to all-on-whom-his-favour-rests.

Never pause before a defining phrase.

To check whether a who / which / that phrase is defining or describing, leave the phrase out of the sentence. If the meaning is still basically the same, it's a describing phrase and you pause. If the meaning is altered or incomplete or lost altogether, it's a defining phrase so don't pause.

On this occasion the Bible translators have made the punctuation helpful. The describing phrase, which should have a pause, has a comma before it: '...the baby, who was lying...' And the defining phrase-that-has-no-pause has no comma: 'peace to all on whom…' But writers don't always get it right, so we need to put 'who / which / phrases to our own test. For instance, in this passage the two 'that' phrases have no commas. But are they describing or defining? I leave you to decide.[10]

> I bring you good news of great joy *that will be for all the people*…
>> Let's go to Bethlehem —
> And see this thing *that has happened*…

Our own judgment

There are two other cases where punctuation won't help us, and we need to decide for ourselves where to put the pauses. These are matters of taste, and different readers will make difference choices.

Where a stretch of words is too long:
For me the sentence 'But Mary treasured up all these things and pondered them in her heart' is too long for a single phrase. I think of Mary's action in two stages: first treasuring things up, then pondering them. So I read it as two phrases:

> But Mary treasured up all these things ´ and pondered them in her heart.

Where you want to emphasise a word:
It is possible to draw attention to a word by pausing before or after it. I have often puzzled over the sign that the angel promises to the shepherds. If he means a clue to help them recognise the Saviour who has just been born, there is nothing very special about a baby wrapped in cloths. What *is* distinctive, and appropriate for them as animal-tenders, is a baby lying in a *manger*. That's the word I want to stress. So this is how I read it.

> This will be a sign to you: ´ You will find a baby wrapped in cloths ´ and lying in a | *[wait for it – this is the bit you must remember]* manger.

'Manger' comes last in the sentence, so I have to put the pause before it, not after. By and large, this sort of emphatic pause should come before the word unless it is the main subject of the sentence – then it should come after the word. If I wanted to draw attention to the chorus of angels and leave you time to visualise them, I would pause after mentioning them because they are the subject of their sentence.

Suddenly a great company of the heavenly host |
appeared with the angel, ´ praising God.

So much for phrases and pauses. Now we move to word-stress and emphasis in their own right.

STRESS

In English we stress some words more than others. (If you try to read a sentence with the same emphasis on every syllable, it sounds ridiculously flat.) This is a natural rhythm of the language from at least as far back as Anglo Saxon poetry, where every phrase had two stresses. We also use stress like the light and shade in a picture, to bring out subconscious layers of meaning. And if you stress the wrong word, you import the wrong meaning. Our story from Luke begins, 'There were shepherds living out in the fields', but if you hit the last word of the sentence too hard – 'keeping watch over their flocks at *night*' – you imply they went home or dozed off in the day. So it is important to stress the right or most suitable words.

For experienced readers this becomes a matter of instinct, and there are no hard and fast rules beyond 'stress words where the meaning wants them stressed'. But there are several helpful guidelines if you want to check that your word-stress is working with the grain of the text and not against it.

Stress words that introduce a new character or event
And soft-pedal words that refer back to things we have already heard about.

An *angel of the Lord [new character]* appeared to them
[the shepherds we've already heard about], and the
glory of the Lord *[we've already had the phrase 'of the
Lord' – soft-pedal it]* shone around them, and they were
terrified.

Stress words that make a contrast

Glory to God in the *highest*
and on *earth* peace to all on whom his favour rests.

Soft-pedal minor words

(Unless they are part of a contrast.) These are the small, less important words which link the major words together. Here are some common examples.

- 'When' is usually hurrying us on to the next event and referring us back to something that has already had emphasis.

  When the angels had left them and gone into heaven...
      When they had seen him...

- 'Thing(s)' – a humble, shorthand word standing in for something else that again we have usually heard about already. The emphasis belongs somewhere else.

  But Mary *[in contrast to 'all who heard what the shepherds said']* treasured up all these things and pondered *[what she did with the things is more important than the things themselves]* them in her heart. The shepherds returned, glorifying and praising God *[again, what they did with the things]* for all the things they had heard and seen...

- Pronouns (he, she, it) once again refer us back to people who have already had their emphasis. Many readers stress '*he* is Christ the Lord', but I think they are wrong. The important thing is *who* he is, not who *he* is!

  Today in the town of David a *Saviour [the new character]* has been born to you; he is *Christ* the Lord.

When an adjective and noun come together...

...decide which is the more noteworthy. Usually it will be the adjective because it's telling you what is special about the noun.

> Suddenly a *great* company of the *heavenly* host appeared
> with the angel, praising God.

But this isn't something to follow slavishly. Sometimes the adjective and noun belong together almost like a single word – you could argue this for 'heavenly host'. Sometimes it is more effective to go against the rhythm and stress the noun. What would you do with 'I bring you good news of great joy'?

Soft-pedal words in brackets

By definition they are less important, almost an afterthought. There are no words in brackets in the Luke story, but I think the very last phrase virtually could be.

> The shepherds returned, glorifying and praising God for
> all the things they had heard and seen, (which were just
> as they had been told).

It is a describing phrase which doesn't seem to add anything important to the story.[11] This is quite a challenge to the reader. It's nice when the story ends with a good strong punchline to ram home. In this case I would fade gently out, but without going so quiet that no one can hear me! When you turn the volume knob down, you need to speak all the more clearly and distinctly.

So you want to be an expert!

VISUAL REINFORCEMENT

If you're not able to act the story out, there are other ways to give people things to look at, which will reinforce its impact. Without going to a full dramatisation, you can wear a piece of clothing or display one or more objects which are a major feature of the story: an example might be five small loaves and two fish. Or you can show pictures with a slide or overhead projector which help set the background or add to the atmosphere. With the Christmas story, for instance, you could project famous paintings of the scenes or more modern cartoon artwork.

Visual actions also show the high store you set on the Bible as God's word. This was why Jesus stood to read the scriptures and the assistant handed the book back and forth with such dignity.

Many churches have the custom of standing to listen to the reading from the Gospel.[12] Some have a procession carrying the Bible from the table to the front of the congregation, a picture of the message coming from God to us. The trouble with any custom, in my mind, is that it gradually becomes an empty habit and people lose sight of what it means. The truth behind these customs is real and they are a good idea. But we need to keep varying or refreshing them to remind people of the truth they are trying to express. For every special service – ideally, for *every* service – ask, does the theme call for some apt way to highlight the Bible reading as the high point?

LEARN IT BY HEART?

Remember the church I mentioned, who give the Bible reading to their gifted reader nearly every week? He learns it by heart, so that he can stand before the congregation each Sunday and tell the story as if it were fresh and exciting news. I think there are good reasons for gifted readers to memorise Bible passages, at least sometimes.

Not everyone has a good memory, but actors learn their parts in plays by heart. Concert musicians often play without the printed music. The stories of the Bible are probably the most powerful in world literature. If we have the ability to learn them, don't we owe them this honour? The story comes alive when we aren't tied to standing at the lectern and looking at the book. And our communication with our hearers improves enormously when we are free to look them in the eye. The better our communication, the more we open the channels for God to speak.

Learning by heart may be too much to manage every week. But it can be valuable for special occasions. A church near where I live makes their readers learn the words for the readings at their Christmas carol service. And I remember going to the Holy Land in a party led by my father-in-law. When we came to Bethlehem, he amazed us by reciting Luke's story of the birth of Jesus from memory. It was, of course, the ideal setting. He brought the Bible story back to life for us as we stood in the place where it happened.

BECOME A BIBLE READING OVERSEER?

You could be just the person to help the quality of Bible reading in your church take a leap forward. There are several ways you could do this:

- Lead and direct dramatised or choral readings.

- Train and develop the gifts of other regular Bible readers, and recruit new ones.

- Concentrate on special occasions yourself – guest services, major festivals, church anniversaries – to allow others full scope on 'ordinary' Sundays.

- Be in charge of the Bible-reading section of all services, choosing who and how to read each passage.

A TEAM OF SPECIALIST BIBLE READERS

The 'Bible supremo' jobs outlined above would go even better if there was a team of you working on them together. You could be a ginger-group or community of Bible people to help the church as a whole keep the Bible at the heart of their life. We are in what's sometimes called a 'post-literate' culture where most people don't read as a major part of their work or leisure. So it is unrealistic to expect them to take naturally to reading the Bible on their own. And it's unnecessary, because there are other ways we can feed them with the Bible. Agencies like Scripture Union or the Bible Society are already into the technological route: putting Bible stories onto cassettes, videos, computer games, and so on. But there is a more basic way for local churches to do it. Most people feel more at home with other people than they do with a book. So give the Bible a human face. Make your expert readers *be* the Bible to their families, home groups and congregations – a human, talking Bible that people can see and hear, rather than pages of print to read.

Of course, *someone* still needs to read the printed Bible to get the words and the stories right. This is where your team comes in. It can include your Bible teachers and others from the minority who love reading to themselves and do it naturally. Some could see their role as students of the word, concentrating on research and being a resource to the others. Even among the 'readers-out-loud', there may be a helpful variety of emphasis. Some might be best at reading and expressing the exact Bible words. People who are housebound or in hospital would love a visit from them. Others may have more of a gift for retelling stories in their own words. They could be wonderful at visiting home groups to tell the Bible story that they will be discussing in their meeting.

THE CHANCE TO READ LONGER PASSAGES

Everything in this chapter so far has assumed the confines of our normal church services. In most places the standard diet is seldom more than fifteen verses per reading (perhaps because the quality of reading is usually so uninspiring). In comparison with earlier generations of Christians, we are seriously undernourishing ourselves. Here, for example, is the oldest account outside the Bible itself of a Christian meeting. We are in Rome around AD150:

> On the day named after the sun, all who live in the countryside or city assemble, and the memoirs of the apostles or the writings of the prophets are read *for as long as time allows.* When the reading is finished, the president addresses us, admonishing us and exhorting us to imitate the splendid things we have heard. Then we all stand and pray...'
>
> *First Apology of Justin Martyr, 67:3–5 (my italics)*

The 'memoirs of the apostles' are the Gospels and perhaps letters from apostles such as Paul, Peter and John. The 'writings of the prophets' probably cover all the Old Testament scriptures. These readings carried on for as long as possible. The president's address depended on them; he applied them to daily living. This is the balance between Bible reading and 'sermon' which I have been arguing for.

The Bible deserves this bigger, more virile share of our meetings. I long for us to give more time and space to the reading in our normal Sunday services. But it may need a programme of special events to show the way and build up an appetite.

One example, where again the balance seems right, is the exciting event recorded in Nehemiah 8, recounting how the Jews celebrated the rebuilding of the temple after their return to Jerusalem. They gathered as many people as they could and simply read the Bible to them. Ezra, the teacher, read the books of Moses from early morning until noon! Meanwhile, there was a simultaneous translation service going on, not into foreign languages but into their own. The Levites 'read from the Book of the

Teachings of God and explained what it meant so the people understood what was being read' (v8).

This seems to me a lovely model for special Bible festivals and we might do well to increase its use at those we already hold. What attention at the moment is given to listening to the Bible text itself being read or dramatised? The odd chapter perhaps. But what a great chance to listen to the Bible in the units in which it was originally written – whole books. Have you ever heard a New Testament letter (longer than Philemon or Jude!) in its original form – that is, read whole? Public readings to the whole assembly could alternate with discussion and prayer groups led by modern 'Levites' helping to explain what the text means for us today.

And what about holidays, weekends or day conferences built round books of the Bible? An Exodus experience perhaps, or a package tour of Acts. Or recreate Nehemiah 8, making use of music, dance and visuals. I have been part of Scripture Union holidays for young people which have done exactly this with Jonah, Genesis 1–11, Philemon, the parable of the sower, the man born blind in John's Gospel, and the early years of King David. My children were in a group who did it with Esther. But this kind of thing could be done by whole churches, not just their youth groups.

Another chance to celebrate Bible stories is in joint services between neighbouring churches of different denominations. Some of our history and customs divide us, but what we have in common is the Bible. A good way to build bridges is to present favourite Bible stories to each other and share what they have come to mean to us.

• Things to do

These ideas are graded at three levels – 'Beginners', 'Growing more experienced' and 'Experts'. Choose the level that is right for you. The activities are a mix of practising your skills, learning from your successes and mistakes, and learning from others. Some you can do on your own, some are better done in a group (eg all the people who regularly do Bible readings in your church).

BEGINNERS
* Choose one of your favourite Bible stories, read it to one or two friends, and tell them why you like it so much.

Then let them do the same for you. Discuss together what tips for reading the Bible aloud this has brought to your minds.

- Practise reading the Bible in your church building. Ask someone you know well, who doesn't make you feel embarrassed, to sit at the back and listen. Ask them to tell you:

  What they enjoy about the way you are reading it.
  Anything they couldn't hear.
  Anything they think might come over better if you read it another way.

- Choose several Bible passages, perhaps the readings for the next few weeks at church if they are already set. Practise writing short introductions to them, which would help listeners to follow them with ease and understanding.

- Practise with Bible names. Work on Nehemiah 3, Matthew 1:1–17 or Luke 3:23–38. Take advice on any names you're not sure of; practise until you don't stumble on them; then read the whole passage aloud confidently, until you at least *sound* as if you know what you're doing!

- Ask someone whose opinion you respect to make comments on your efforts at reading.

- Ask someone more experienced – perhaps the person who organises Bible reading in your church – to work with you on the next reading you do. Perhaps they could help you prepare and practise or, better still, share the reading with you.

GROWING MORE EXPERIENCED
- Take the story of Naaman (2 Kings 5) or part of the Christmas story (other than Luke 2:8–20). Prepare to give a reading of it by working in detail on expression,

phrasing and word-stress (or, to begin with, just one of them). Use a copy of the text you don't mind marking.

- Again, take the story of Naaman or part of the Christmas story or, better still, take the reading for an all-age service which will be happening soon in your church. Try rewriting it as a response story for the congregation to join in (see pp101–102). Test it on a sample of church members. If it goes well, offer to lead the story when the time comes.

- Once you have done a reading, don't forget all about it. Review it by going through your copy of the text again. Ask yourself:

  Was there any moment when I could see that listeners were finding it difficult to follow?
  Was there any evidence that the reading came alive for them?
  How far did I succeed in lifting the words off the page by using expression, phrasing and word-stress?
  What should I learn from this to improve my reading?
  What should I remember to do (or not do) next time?

- Listen to a tape of the Bible being read. Pay special attention to the expression, phrasing and word-stress. What can you learn from it? Are there ideas and approaches you could adapt the next time you read?

- Listen carefully to the television or radio news. See how the readers and reporters handle expression, phrasing and word-stress. Most of the time they do it well, but sometimes they make a right mess of it. Even professionals need to keep learning and improving. What can we learn from their good (and bad) practice?

EXPERTS
- Work on expression, phrasing and word-stress with some demanding passages. Two good examples would be

Matthew 23 (a long speech from Jesus) and John 1:1–18 (the hardest Christmas reading – be careful to apply the guidelines on pp112–114 to verses 1 and 2).

- Plan how to read Matthew 22:15–46 dramatically with a team of readers, or chorally using the whole congregation. Practise to see how it works.

- Choose a Bible story, ideally one you are planning to read at church soon, and either learn it by heart or decide how else you might reinforce it visually for the hearers. If possible, when the time comes, go ahead and do it like that in church.

- Listen to yourself on tape or watch yourself on video. What effective moments do you notice which you can build on and develop? What mannerisms would it be better to iron out?

- Watch one or more of Philip Sherlock's video retellings of Bible stories for Scripture Union (*Joseph*, *Exodus* and *All or Nothing* [about Paul]). What can you learn from them? What could you try the next time you tell a Bible story?

- Watch other people reading the Bible, at your own church or elsewhere. What do they do well? How would you advise and guide them to do better?

• Quotes

The church is where the stories of Israel and Jesus are told, enacted and heard, and it is our conviction that as a Christian people there is literally nothing more important we can do.

Stanley Hauerwas, The Peaceable Kingdom,
University of Notre Dame Press, 1983, pp 99–100

I am convinced that using a lectionary – reading the Bible in little snippets – is a second-order activity; the

primary activity ought to be reading the Bible in large
chunks, to get its full flavour and thrust.

Tom Wright, Following Jesus, SPCK, 1994, p x

A man with an unsmiling face stood at the dimly-lit
lectern of the large church. In the sing-song-not-ordinary
voice many use in preaching, he read from the Bible. The
congregation sat politely silent. The sonorous voice
droned on. The listeners' attention was lost after the
first few verses. His 'reverent' but monotonous voice finished. 'Here endeth the second lesson.'

The reading was over – and forgotten.

The same words read as they are meant to be are living,
powerful, surgically sharp and effective. But it means work.

Another man spent two hours preparing the chapter
to be read. There was a glow inside him when he real-
ized that the meaning of the passage was clearer in his
mind than ever before.

He marked his Bible for emphasis and pauses, read
the chapter, recording it on his cassette player and playing it back to himself. As he did this his pen marked one
place where he had overlooked a contrast, another
where a pause would make the meaning clearer.

In the church his face was relaxed in a smile, his eyes
greeted his listeners as he told them the book and chapter from which he was reading. (He had checked the
microphone before the service.)

People listened as he read clearly, enthusiastically in a
normal voice. They heard, understood and appreciated as
their ears and eyes were held by a reader who loved
God and his word and prepared the reading as carefully
as he would a talk.

Clifford Warne, Paul White and Annie Vallotton,
Using the Bible for Reading Out Loud, pp 39–40

• Resources

BRINGING THE BIBLE TO LIFE

In the early 1980s the actor Alec McCowen created a sensation by
reciting Mark's Gospel on stage. I went to see him in London's

Mermaid Theatre, and found the evening just as riveting as my visit to the English-speaking church in Holland nearly twenty years earlier. Alec was proving that the Bible story is totally captivating – anywhere, not just in church. As I sat watching, I once again knew this was something I wanted to do. Well, not just 'wanted' – I burnt to do it, burning (I hoped) with passion for God's cause. It stung me that Alec wasn't a committed Christian. Surely it would be better to have the Bible performed by someone who revered the gospel story as God's truth.

In 1986 I launched myself as a Bible reciter at a youth evangelistic evening in High Wycombe. Instead of a 20-minute talk, I acted out two stories from The Acts of the Apostles: Paul's conversion, and his later sermon in Athens. I noticed that, unlike when I spoke my own words, there was no problem in holding people's attention – the Bible stories were gripping. I included a story from Acts in every meeting I took that year.

In 1987 I worked up a 35-minute sequence and performed it at the Edinburgh and Greenbelt Festival fringes. The following April I launched my full 90-minute selection of the highlights of Acts at the Nationwide Evangelical Anglican Celebration. This was at Caister Holiday Camp in Norfolk, where spring seems to arrive later than in the rest of the country. It was so cold, I had to learn the words through chattering teeth. The only place I could find empty was a marquee before breakfast. But at least nobody could see me – I was wearing wellingtons because of the wet grass and a sleeping bag wrapped round the rest of my clothes!

Since then I have added three other Bible recitals to my repertoire: the Elijah story from the Old Testament, a New Testament letter, 1 Thessalonians, with special attention to the story behind it, and 'The Sixty-Minute Bible', a race through the main stories of the Bible in one hour! I have a season each year when I offer to perform these Bible one-man shows for churches, schools, conferences and arts festivals.

For further information about 'Bringing the Bible to life', contact the author at **48 Peterborough Road, London SW6 3EB**.

• Notes

1   The Bible reading usually comes before the sermon, and this seems sensible, especially if the sermon is based on

it (as I suggest it should be). But in fact there may often be a case for having the Bible reading after the sermon instead, or perhaps both before *and* after. When the preacher has explained it in detail, *then* we are ready to hear it clearly and understand it.

2   Teachers sat down to encourage questions and discussion (Luke 2:46). But scripture readers stood up to proclaim God's word: they expected no interruption.

3   2 Kings 5:15–27 (Old Testament, pp352–353), *Good News Bible* dramatised text, from *The Dramatised Bible* © 1989 Michael Perry, Marshall Pickering. Text © 1966, 1971, 1976 American Bible Society.

4   Luke 2:8–14 (New Testament, pp124–125), *New International Version* dramatised text from *The Dramatised Bible* © 1989 Michael Perry, Marshall Pickering. Text © 1973, 1978, 1984 by International Bible Society.

Of course you don't have to use the arrangement in *The Dramatised Bible*. You can make your own dramatisation of any Bible passage. And even when you use *The Dramatised Bible* script, you can adapt it: for instance, leave out 'he said' when it isn't necessary and, if the Narrator's part is large, share it among two or three readers.

5   Luke 24:50–53; Acts 1:10–11 (*Good News Bible*).

6   The story of Easter would work well, but not Good Friday. Otherwise, most well-known Bible stories lend themselves to this treatment, especially Jesus' parables. If you're still not sure, look at a book of drama scripts based on Bible stories. If they make a good humorous sketch, they will be ideal as response stories. See Note 7 below.

7   'Gideon' from *Acting Up*, by Dave Hopwood, National Society / Church House Publishing, 1995, pp85–86,

copyright © Dave Hopwood, reproduced by permission. This book also contains response stories on Nehemiah, the Wise Men at Christmas and the Easter story.

8 In this section I have developed ideas from Anna de Lange, 'The reading today' (Administry's Adminisheet 33) and Clifford Warne, Paul White and Annie Vallotton, *Using the Bible for Reading Out Loud* (Bible Society, 1980).

9 The word 'phrase' is used loosely here and not in its strict grammatical sense. In this chapter the words 'phrase' and 'phrasing' are referring to groups of words which help make up the rhythm of speech.

10 Well, at least have a try. In case you can't decide, I think 'good news of great joy *that will be for all the people*' (Luke 2:10) is a *describing* phrase: you could leave the phrase out without affecting the meaning. But 'see this thing *that has happened*' (v15) seems to me to be a *defining* phrase: without it, we wouldn't be altogether sure what 'thing' the shepherds were talking about.

11 This will depend on the wider setting of the service you are reading this story in. Taking the story on its own, this closing phrase sounds unimportant. But, of course, if you're in a carol service where all the readings are stressing that God planned and foretold the coming of Jesus over many centuries, the phrase takes on a vital thrust.

12 However, it is fair to ask, why only stand for the Gospel reading? Are we implying that it is more important than readings from the Old Testament or the epistles? And if so, is that what we really mean?

The story goes on,
and on...

This has been a book about telling stories in churches. That's good because churches should be storytelling communities.

But churches should not be the only place where Christians tell stories. The world around us needs to hear God's stories – the good news of Jesus himself, stories of what he is doing in the lives of his friends and followers, and good wholesome stories that make life richer. Perhaps this is the raw material for another book.

For now, let me leave you with a plea and with news of a helpful resource. The plea is for us all to offer God our love of stories and see what he wants to make of it. For me at the moment, this means exploring whether I can write short stories for secular magazines. Stories that express Christian feelings and values, and take them where no other Christian writing can get through. And if I haven't got the ability to do it, perhaps you have. Or perhaps there's some quite different way God can use you to tell stories beyond the circle of your Christian friends.

Meanwhile, there is a project trying to do this very thing with the Bible's stories. Is there some way you and your church could get involved?

THE OPEN BOOK

The Open Book is an initiative of Churches Together in England and Bible Society, timed to make an impact as the twentieth century closes and the new millennium dawns. The 'open book' is the Bible, and the project seeks to engage the churches and the wider culture with key biblical themes and stories in dynamic new ways. One of the project's slogans is 'Opening the book to the people, and the people to the book'. This works has three aims:

1   To increase awareness, knowledge and understanding of
    the Bible in the public domain.

2   To re-establish the credibility of the Bible in the public
    domain.

3   To engender a more credible, life-giving encounter with
    scripture as the story of God's interaction with his world.

The overriding objective behind these aims is to ensure that the
story informs what is going on in key areas of cultural change –
ie the debate in politics, the media, education and the creative arts
– and therefore contributes to the ongoing concerns about what
kind of society we want to be part of in the twenty-first century.
So another slogan for the project is 'Telling the story to shape
tomorrow'.

Because the Bible consists of both a story and stories, The
Open Book will focus on five or six Bible stories related to key
Christian themes:

The Creation (Identity)
Good Friday/Easter (Forgiveness)
Exodus (Freedom)
Exile & Restoration (Justice)
The Nativity (Hope)

…with the story of Joseph probably forming an over-arching
introduction to all these themes.

The project will encourage the telling of these stories through
a variety of means – storytelling, musicals, debate, creative arts,
multimedia and information technology, theatre, video, interactive presentations and other media – at local, regional and national
levels. These events are due to begin in 1998.

For further information, including how to order a church
resource pack, contact **The Open Book, PO Box 1100, Stonehill
Green, Westlea, Swindon SN5 7DG, tel 01793 418100 or 24-hr
information line 01793 418152**.